In the Hands of the Arabs

CAPTAIN E. L. BUCHANAN

In the Hands of the Arabs

An Airman's Wife in Mesopotamia
Post the First World War

Zetton Buchanan

LEONAUR

In the Hands of the Arabs
An Airman's Wife in Mesopotamia Post the First World War
by Zetton Buchanan

First published under the title
In the Hands of the Arabs

Leonaur is an imprint of Oakpast Ltd

ISBN: 978-0-85706-733-3 (hardcover)
ISBN: 978-0-85706-734-0 (softcover)

http://www.leonaur.com

Publisher's Notes

Contents

DEDICATED TO THE MEMORY OF
SOME VERY GALLANT GENTLEMEN
CAPTAIN J. T. BRADFIELD, 1/4 SOMERSET L.I.
CAPTAIN W. T. WRIGLEY, M.C., LATE 5TH WILTS
AND
MY HUSBAND
CAPTAIN E. L. BUCHANAN, LATE R.A.F.

Preface

This is the true story of the tragedy of the lonely outpost in Mesopotamia—that country of wonderful possibilities.

I write my story as I would tell it, and I have no fluent and gifted pen to help me in my task; therefore, for any shortcomings I must ask my readers' forgiveness.

The glorious deaths of these young heroes, so full of life and promise, brings so forcibly back to me that—

Those whom the Gods love die young,
And those whose heart is dry as summer dust,
Burn to the socket.

BANK STREET, BAGHDAD (LOOKING TOWARDS EXCHANGE SQUARE).

NORTHERN ENTRANCE TO BAZAARS. BAGHDAD.

CHAPTER 1

My Introduction to Mesopotamia

It was on the 17th of May 1920 that I arrived at Basrah, *via* Bombay, to join my husband at his post with the Irrigation Department in Mesopotamia. It seemed to me hours before the boat came alongside the quay and Billy ran up to greet me. Though we had only been separated five months it had seemed ages, and we were overjoyed at seeing each other.

Then began the business of moving my luggage, which ultimately arrived in Shahraban more or less intact. When I got off the boat myself, I found a car waiting to take me to the station, and a motor-lorry and bullock-cart behind to bring the luggage.

I was really thrilled when I first set foot on Mesopotamian soil. 'What glorious sand! Wouldn't John love it?' was my first thought. There was a most wonderful sunset, and I watched it spell-bound all the way to the station. The colourings were gorgeously brilliant that evening, and I never saw the sun set like this before or since. Next, the station—and the mass of things which Billy had brought me for the journey. There were plenty of iced drinks, and food enough for a week's travel, fruit, chocolates, magazines, cushions, etc., etc. I was enchanted with everything—except, perhaps, the dinner, which we had in a tent beside the station. It was not appetising.

The train started at eight o'clock, and we settled ourselves down for a twenty-five hours' journey. The Basrah-Baghdad railway had only been completed a few weeks, and this train, unfortunately, was not one of the best running. But we were so happy to see each other again that we were quite ready to overlook anything that was not quite up to the mark.

Of course Billy was very disappointed that I had not brought our baby John, as I had intended right up to the week before I sailed. In fact, I had even had everything for him packed. People at home, however, told me that it was most unwise to take a baby out to Mesopotamia in the hot weather, and my mother-in-law at last prevailed upon me to leave him behind in her care; but it was an awful wrench, for he was at the adorable age of fifteen months.

Another disappointment was the non-arrival of my dog 'Wu-Wu,' whom Billy had fully expected to come out with me. I had meant to bring him, too, but before I sailed everybody told me that a Pekinese had no chance in Mesopotamia. When I arrived I felt very sorry I had not both John and Wu-Wu with me; but the next day I was thankful. The following morning, when the train stopped for passengers to breakfast, our cook made a delicious meal by the wayside. He set up two bricks first and put a frying-pan on the top, some wood underneath. I did not care to watch the process, as I was sure the result would be smoky. But when breakfast arrived, there was nothing to grumble about. The train stopped for about thirty minutes and then restarted. It was terrifically hot, and the sand blew through the wire-gauze in the open windows and smothered everything; but I had to have the shutters down on each side, so as not to miss the scenery.

Billy explained each place to me as we passed it, and what had happened there. I was most excited when I saw the first string of camels on the horizon. There were miles and miles of desert sand, dotted here and there with stunted shrubs, and in the far distance the camels. I was so enchanted with it all that Billy thought it necessary to warn me that I should get fed up with such things after a time, but I was certain that I never should. Next a horseman came galloping across the desert, his *abba*—a long, flowing, *kimono*-shaped cloak, worn by the Arabs, both men and women—blown out by the wind like a sail. He reminded me of pictures I had seen, and only his lance was missing. He seemed a mere atom in proportion to the vast waste of sand.

Another stop came. The train slowed down at a 'station '; but there was no platform. We halted for lunch in a tent. Our bearer stopped in our carriage while we were gone, to see that no one stole our property. The food was horrid, served on enamelled tin plates, with aluminium forks and spoons, which put me still more against it. Wonderfully cold iced drinks, however, were a compensation.

We went on after lunch towards Hillah, the country growing more and more fertile as we neared it. Clumps of date-palms and numerous fruit-gardens could be seen. Billy pointed out the remains of some old canals used thousands of years ago.

I was not very impressed with the canals. I was more interested in the little Arab children who stood by and waved at the train as it passed. But oh, how dirty they looked, and their clothing seemed mostly nondescript rags!

We arrived at Hillah, or rather Hillah Station. A crowd of Arabs was waiting about for the train. The women were all closely veiled, so I could not see whether they were beautiful or not. They certainly had not the lovely eyes which I had expected.

Hillah itself in the distance looked very fertile. The date-palms were innumerable, and everything about it had a cool and refreshing appearance. (There are other tales about it; I have heard it called the last place God ever made!)

I drank my first Arab tea here, served in a short little glass, with no milk, but abundance of sugar. It is a tea one gets to like very much in time. After about half an hour's wait we re-entered the train, and as the sun began to set we started for Baghdad. Baghdad! What's in a name? A tremendous lot. That name had always conjured up for me the vision of a city of dazzling splendour, full of Arabian Nightish romance and lovely women, *bazaars* teeming with life and colour. Certainly I expected too much!

It was 9 p.m. when we arrived, and everything was dim and vague. Small groups of Arabs stood about everywhere, gesticulating, chattering, occasionally quarrelling, all adding to the noise, which was already deafening. However, the Director of Irrigation and his wife were waiting for us, and, as a strong wind was blowing, I was quickly taken to their billet, while my husband saw to the luggage.

The ride in the car from the station to the billet was full of interest. Everything was so novel to me, and by night all seemed so big. The date-palms were enormous. But oh the dust! Soon after we were indoors a terrific sandstorm arose. All the shutters of the billet were closed, yet the sand got through. The wind howled outside and slapped up against the shutters. I began to get very worried about my husband. When he did come he was smothered in sand; but he declared that this was nothing, and that the luggage was all safe.

Our host's billet was very nice—one of the best in Baghdad, Billy afterwards told me; and he warned me not to expect ours in Shahraban to be anything like this.

On the following day we went to see the *bazaars*. Everything looked totally different by daylight. We passed down New Street, the one broad main street of the place, which is the only road suitable for traffic in our sense of the word. The traffic was mostly Ford cars, donkeys with most cumbersome loads, and numbers of ponies carrying either riders or merchandise.

We left the car at the entrance of one of the *bazaars* and made our way through the narrow opening which led directly into the interior. My first overwhelming sensation was the mingled odours of human beings, tannin, and the refuse of ages. The *bazaar* was like a warren, little streets or alleys branching off in all directions. The vendors sat in small cone-shaped doorways with their goods displayed around them, calling out to all who passed to come and bay. Of course it is quite an art for a Briton to purchase any article at a reasonable price unless he speaks Arabic fluently.

I looked for the blaze of brilliant oriental colour which I had expected to find. I sought in vain for any wonderfully coloured silks; they were not to be found. But the natives have spoilt the atmosphere by doing their utmost to cater for 'the English.' Practically anything is procurable, from stickphast and stationery to genuine old Persian rugs, which seemed far more in place than those Western products.

The hum and jostle passed all expectation. The noise in the brass *bazaar* was the worst. The chink of the brass being beaten or of rivets being put in necessitated our shouting to be heard.

There were a few Arab women about, all closely veiled but mostly wearing black, doing their bargaining as well as, or better than, the men.

The *bazaars* are covered in overhead in a series of arches, mostly of matting and mud, but every now and then is an open space through which the scorching sun pours and an occasional minaret can be seen, set as it were in a frame.

We wandered on and seemed to have walked miles. On those floors, which are merely hardened mud and are full of ruts and holes, it was a weary task getting along, and I began to realise what the heat really meant. It was a good thing that we had a guide with us, for we should never have found our way back to the car without him. I had been allowed to choose my own direction in our wanderings, and had quite lost my bearings.

We left as early as 5.30 the next morning to catch the train leaving Baghdad East for Shahraban, which we expected to reach at 11 a.m. Our carriage was a covered-in iron truck, quite empty except for our own chairs, which we took with us. Our first stop was at Cassel's Post, not far from Baghdad. Then came Coningham's Post; then the refugee camp, Baqubah, where the Armenians and Nestorian Christians had been put for protection; and then Baqubah itself, a delightful-looking place from the train. There were green fruit-gardens and belts of date-palms all round the town, and the Diyalah River could be seen, where buffaloes lazed with just their heads and backbones above water.

I was enchanted with the view of Baqubah; but Billy assured me that the Shahraban gardens were stunning and far better than Baqubah's, though of course the Baqubah people thought their vegetation much superior to Shahraban's.

Next came Abu Hawa, and then Abu Jisrah, which is famous for its oranges. And, at last, we were really in sight of Shahraban. It appeared splendidly green and refreshing, and I felt how good it was to have come here. I told Billy what a lovely place it looked and that I was dying to get inside the town. I meant it too. It must be remembered that I was very happy and pleased with life in general, and saw everything with the eyes of an optimist!

Billy pointed out Table Mountain in the distance and gave most glowing accounts of it, what a gorgeous place it was, and what excellent bathing could be had. But Shahraban itself interested me most— and now we had reached it.

CHAPTER 2

My New Home

There was a little crowd of Arabs waiting to fetch the luggage at Shahraban Station. The weights they carried on their backs were remarkable. The way that they manage is like this. A cord is passed round a box and round the men's foreheads, and the hands are used to steady the burden. Some of my crates and trunks, however, were too much even for the strongest Arab to tackle; and a bullock-cart had to be requisitioned.

We walked from the station to our billet, a matter of about a mile and a half. It was very hot, though only May. But I enjoyed walking, as I could take in the details so much better. The road from the station for the first half-mile was heavy sand, and huge black ants were busily engaged running backwards and forwards over it. Then the road, or track, narrowed, and there were high mud walls to protect the gardens from anyone who might take a fancy to the fruit. Quaint little wooden gates studded with iron bolts were to be seen at intervals along the walls. Then we entered the town. The streets were very narrow. Quantities of dirt and refuse were thrown up in corners. On either side there were mud houses, with merely a door in the lower storey. The upper storeys had picturesque old latticed windows built out so that they overhung the road. There seemed very few people about. A handful of women were washing clothes in a stream, and some children were playing in the road.

We turned a corner, and suddenly came upon our billet. It was an Arab house, and I cannot say that I was very impressed with the exterior. The walls were of plain mud, without a break, apart from the doorway, on the lower floor. In the upper storey were windows with wooden shutters, and half-way up a quaint overhanging latticed wooden window, with tiny panes of glass in the upper part.

I was going in, but could not pass the door without admiring it. It was an enormous, massive piece of wood, with great iron studs dotted all over it; and what a keyhole! The key was brought for my inspection—a great heavy iron thing, a foot long—and we went in. The servants were standing in the passage, which was dome-shaped above with a brick floor below.

In the hall there were three more doors, one leading to a back staircase, which went up to a verandah; another to a *surdab*,[1] which was used as an office for the Indian clerk; and the third led into the court-yard. This was square, the floor of great square bricks, and wooden pillars, elaborately carved at the top, supporting the verandah. There was a little patch of earth in it, in which stood one solitary palm-tree. I thought of all the seeds I had brought stored away in a trunk, and determined that in a short time I would have a pretty little garden.

I went all round inspecting, to the great delight of my husband, who had spent much time and money in getting things comfortable for me. The first door on the left of the courtyard led to the clerk's office, which was delightfully cool. Then came Billy's own office, a very business-like looking room, with a beautiful arched ceiling. Next a large *surdab*, which I immediately furnished in my mind's eye. It was then almost empty, except for a bench, camp-bed, and *punkah*. The brick ceiling had three fine domes. The walls were of mud and brick, and Billy had had them plastered over in places, so as to make them level.

Next to this room, and leading from it through a little archway, was a smaller *surdab*, which was very high and had but little furniture in it. The servants' quarters came next, and then a fine long room, evidently intended for a stable, but at this time full of rubbish and badly in need of repair. Lastly there was the store-room, admirably supplied with shelves; and the kitchen, which I at once decided to have thoroughly cleaned out and whitewashed.

Then Billy said he wanted me to come upstairs—which stairs were very steep mud steps. If I had been pleased with the ground floor, I was still more pleased with the upper. It was really splendid. The dining-room had three windows in very deep recesses, and a fine fireplace, which Billy had had put in. The walls were painted with mud, beautifully done and looking like fawn distemper, and there was a white frieze and picture-rail round the room. Little cupboards with well-fitted shelves were let into the wall. The floor was of brick.

1. The name given to the rooms situated on the ground floor.

Next to this room was a small bedroom, square, with two windows looking out on the road, and a wooden partition with glass in the upper half cutting it off from the verandah overlooking the courtyard. In the centre of the ceiling was a quaint decoration of coloured glass. Then came our bedroom, with which I was delighted. Its windows overhanging the road, had a big *chick* [2] outside to keep off the sun, and there was also a *punkah* to secure coolness. It had two doors and a wooden window facing the verandah. The floor was of square bricks, and there was a decorated ceiling.

I was anxious to start unpacking at once and begin arranging the house. Billy, however, made me first have lunch and a rest, though I did not feel in the least tired. It was not until the following day that the unpacking began, and then there was great excitement. The servants' faces were studies as each trunk was opened. They were quite as enthusiastic as we were, and expressed great admiration for all the European things.

I found that I had brought plenty of everything—camp-chairs, little tables, quantities of cushions, cooking utensils, Christmas decorations (and puddings), stores, china, glass, books, a sewing-machine, a shot-gun, tennis-rackets, etc., etc.—in fact, all except heavy furniture. The only thing I seemed to have forgotten was a lemon-squeezer.

It was fortunate that I had brought so much with me, for when I arrived there was a minimum of furniture in the billet—obviously a man's house! It took me over two months to get quite straight. The dining-room looked delightful when finished. Billy designed the furniture and sent the measurements and had the woodwork made in the *bazaar*. The sofa and easy-chairs were stuffed with wool and I covered them with chintz. The absence of springs was hardly noticeable. The walls were hung with carpets, and there was a big *durrey* on the floor with rugs thrown over it. Numbers of cushions and 'humpties' were about the room. The table was a perpetual eyesore to me, being like an ordinary kitchen one. But I always kept the vases well filled with flowers, scarce as they were at this time of year, and when all my ornaments, etc., were out the place looked really attractive.

I had decided that the dining-room should be English, the other rooms Oriental. Coming straight out from the west, Eastern things appealed to me so much more, though women who have lived east long love to make their surroundings as Western as possible.

The big bedroom was rather an effort, and was the last room fin-

2. Sun screen.

ished; but after shelves had been put up, and hangings over them, and I had spent many hours at the machine on curtains, etc., it was a great success. The smaller bedroom, usually my dressing-room, but available as a spare bedroom, looked very dainty when completed. I had brought out yards of mosquito netting, which was quite useless owing to the mesh being too big. I turned it, therefore, into curtains for the walls and a hanging for the door. Gaily coloured divans and some rugs were on the floor, and there was an abundance of bright cushions from England, of a type which we fondly imagine to be Oriental. Then there were numerous knick-knacks and cherished treasures of mine, and photos of John. The only actual furniture was a dressing-table, a writing-table, and some chairs.

Outside on the verandah Billy had arranged a big awning and *chicks* to let down. This we called the verandah-room, but we never used it much. It was always so hot, though it served to keep the heat off the bedrooms.

Upstairs was the roof, just an ordinary flat mud roof such as one finds on any Arab house; but Billy had had a low mud wall built round for John's safety. Here we sat in the evenings. I never grew tired of the view, with the storks—thousands of storks lived in Shahraban and were never disturbed by the Arabs—building their nests on the roofs or the walls, quite fearless of everyone. Then when the Arabs had their principal meal, which is in the evening, smoke arose from almost every house around, giving a misty, unreal effect to the town in the glow of the setting sun. It is impossible to describe those sunsets. The glorious colours were always changing, but were always enchanting to watch. Sometimes I did water-colour sketches of them from the roof, hoping to catch that picture of the town at the moment the sun touched the horizon. For about three minutes it was perfect, with the minaret of the local mosque and the palm-trees standing out against the sky. How one always wished to keep back the departing sun, so as to enjoy the picture a little longer.

I very soon settled down in the billet. At first, of course, I missed my little John badly. But as it grew hotter, I was most thankful I had not brought him out with me. There were so many small difficulties out in the districts which could not have been overcome with a baby.

I have not yet described the servants. There was the Indian bearer who had met the boat at Basrah. Then an Indian cook, to whose lot it generally fell to go periodically to Baghdad to get fresh stores, which were practically unobtainable in Shahraban. We had later two Armenians, procured from the Refugee Camp at Baqubah. One was my maid, and the other the house-boy. The latter, whose name was Gosdan, enters a good deal into this story. He was about seventeen years of age and spoke English. Lastly an Arab *syce* and an Arab sweeper.

Takahe, the Armenian maid, was of course the servant with whom I had most to do. Her duties were to wait on me personally and do the laundry. This last was a very sore point before her arrival. It was just done by a woman in the town, and used to come back unironed. Then I had an Arab woman to come to the house and wash. She was very old, almost blind, and exceedingly dirty. She was very annoyed that I made her rinse the soap out of the clothes—a thing they never do. I found afterwards that she was a very rich woman and owned one of the fruit-gardens; yet she would come and wash for me at the rate of two *annas* an article! Takahe, when she arrived, was more or less of a success, but somewhat lazy. The only time when she displayed energy was while helping me dress for dinner. She was very pleased with the process, and when I was ready she always went a little distance away, put her head on one side, looked me up and down, and generally approved.

There were other inmates of the house, not human. First there was a little pie (or pariah) puppy, who was given me by one of the Sisters at Baqubah Camp. I will say no more of him now, as there will be much to say later. He was at first our only domestic animal. But there were many others not domesticated—the storks on our roof; a whole colony of swallows, which had built their nests in our big *surdab* downstairs, and, until they left us about the end of June, flew freely about the room and perched on the *punkah* and its rope, even when it was being pulled; and, much less pleasing guests, hosts of horrible scorpions. The scorpions were all over the billet, but their headquarters were the barn on the ground floor. When this eventually was turned out, and the refuse of five years got rid of, the haul was tremendous. I got quite expert at catching stray specimens. If one put two together in a jamjar, they would generally fight furiously until one was killed. I do not know whether the servants thought that this scorpion-fighting was a pastime of mine; but they were always bringing me offerings of 'very big scorpion.'

As for neighbours, naturally we saw little of these. There was a coffee-shop opposite, which attracted crowds in the evening; and next to the coffee-shop a house in which it was only too obvious that the residents were women of ill repute. A hideous hag, lame of foot, seemed to be in charge, and the damsels themselves were not at all beautiful, though one, who was taller than the average Arab woman, certainly had wonderful eyes. They went unveiled, and generally sat on the step of their house, laughing and chatting with visitors to the coffee-shop. Later the sound of cymbals and singing could be heard in their courtyard. But at the end, when they moved to the roof, my husband always insisted that we should move our chairs to the other side of our roof, which did not overlook theirs.

We had but one fellow-Englishman in Shahraban, Captain W. T. Wrigley, the Assistant Political officer in the town. I had heard lots about him from Billy before I met him. He had described him as an awfully nice man; and so I found him from the very first. He had charming manners, the kindest of hearts, and that wonderful asset, a sense of humour, as one soon found out when one got to know him.

So here were we three English people living peacefully amid a population of Arabs. Occasional visitors passing through would come to see us; but we always managed to get up enough amusement among ourselves to prevent our ever being bored. Billy's days were mostly like this: Rise 4.30 to 5 a.m., go out to inspect the canals until 8, then breakfast, and afterwards office work till 1 o'clock. *Tiffin.*[3] Rest from 2 to 4. Office work till 5, and then generally free for the rest of the evening, though there were often times when he sat up working until midnight.

My daily programme at the billet was generally as follows: Rise 5 a.m. and see to the house (which I thoroughly enjoyed, as I was able to practise my little bit of Arabic on the servants) until 8. After breakfast, give out the stores, personally superintend the boiling of the milk and drinking-water, sew, etc. *Tiffin.* Rest all the afternoon, and in the evening go out with Billy for a walk or a ride.

I looked forward to the evenings very much. At first we took walks, for it was a fortnight or more before Billy bought me a horse. He could not get a suitable one at once. The one he gave me did not prove an over-safe mount, as will be seen. His own horse was an army one.

A tennis-court was being made when I arrived, situated in a field near the Qeshlah and the graveyard. It took some little time to finish; but when it was ready it proved well worth waiting for. It was made of straw and mud, mixed and thoroughly baked by the sun until it was

3. Lunch.

CAMEL CARAVAN OUTSIDE SHAHRABAN.

DESERT TENT OF BLACK GOAT-HAIR.

hard. Then a layer of very fine mud was put on the top and smoothed out. It was an excellent court.

We would walk down to Captain Wrigley's billet and call for him on our way to tennis. There was always a great commotion when my little Scut met Wrigley's two dogs, 'Girlie' and 'Bint.' They would all dash off excitedly along what we termed the 'Shahraban Promenade,' a road with a tiny stream of water flowing on one side, which seemed the evening promenade-ground of all the dogs in Shahraban. Our dogs then raced along this, and Scut always appeared to feel himself a hero on such occasions.

Both my husband and Captain Wrigley played a splendid game of tennis, and I found myself rather weak in comparison, so I often insisted that they should play singles together.

On our walks there was plenty to be seen—and heard. About half a mile from the billet was a marsh, where the croaking of frogs was terrific. When I first heard the sound, in the billet, I thought it was a train shunting. I would not believe it was frogs until Billy took me for a walk one evening to convince me. Sure enough, there were the frogs in the marsh, and hundreds of storks standing in it, very busily employed. The noise was deafening, and in spite of the storks' efforts it did not seem to decrease.

Then the fire-flies! These I only saw when we were returning later than usual. There were swarms of them flying over the canal, their lamps all brilliantly lit; and most fascinating they were to watch.

The first sight I had of a caravan at Shahraban was quite early in the morning. I remember it well. I heard camel-bells in the distance, and round the bend in the road came the caravan. Some of the camels were laden with merchandise, others had a kind of wicker-box on either side, in which closely- veiled women sat, while the men walked alongside. I was really thrilled at the sight. The same evening we came across another caravan grazing. I told Billy I must have a ride. An Arab selected a camel which he had been riding, and it knelt down. I got on, but in the process of rising was nearly thrown off, and after a few steps I wanted to get off—much to the surprise of the Arabs, who then showed me how it should be done.

Sometimes we went through the gardens. In May and June there were gorgeous apricots, the trees being bowed down with the weight of the fruit. Later came peaches, nectarines, water-melons, figs green and black, grapes, apples, and tiny pears and wonderful pomegranates. To walk through these gardens, picking the sun-kissed fruit as one goes, is ideal.

Compared with fruit, vegetables were poor in Shahraban. Billy got me an allotment in the garden of one of the townspeople, Fahal by name. This was a great excitement to me, as in a short time there was quite a variety of vegetables from which to choose, spinach predominating.

As for my flower-garden at the billet, I felt sure that by September I should have quite a good show. According to the setting out of the seeds there should have been a glow of colour, though there were a few bare patches which left much to be desired.

I very soon grew to love the billet and its surroundings, with the magnificent view of the Persian hills in the distance.

CHAPTER 3

Table Mountain and Quizil Robat

The life out in Shahraban seemed to me ideal. We did not suffer from monotony, and, with the billet as our headquarters, there was the constant excitement for me of going to different places with Billy on his rounds.

The place which I liked the best of all was Table Mountain, about seven miles north of Shahraban. It was just below Table Mountain that the head-works of the Shahraban and other canals were situated, the water running off from the Diyalah River; and in consequence Billy had to pay frequent visits there. We varied the journey, sometimes going by train, which meant a long and tiring walk from the station in the hottest time of the day and over loose sand and stones, which made progress very slow; and at others riding over, far the more delightful way, sending only our luggage by train.

When we reached our destination, Table Mountain was to me a most enjoyable place. Some people, I suppose, would call it barren and desolate; and no doubt to those who only knew it under war conditions it was so, but I did not find it like that. The irrigation huts where we stayed were at the foot of the *Jebel Hamrin* (Red Mountains), and the Diyalah ran past them. The huts themselves were of mud, three built together being used as bedrooms, one large one near as a dining-room, and another some little distance away as a kitchen. Bundles of reed tied together were stood against the door of the big room and water was thrown on them constantly, which made a cool breeze. Also there was a *punkah*, which was occasionally pulled, though there was always a difficulty in getting a boy to pull for any length of time.

Everything that we wanted at Table Mountain had to be brought with us. Our food was therefore mostly tinned, the only local eatables being fruit and vegetables procured half a mile away, where an Arab

25

had a little plot of ground. We had to bring also crockery, cooking utensils, firewood, beds, and chairs, the only furniture which the huts contained being tables. This sounds a terrible business; but it was really no trouble. The servants packed everything, and all I did was to go round with a list of articles likely to be forgotten and see that they were put in.

After getting to Table Mountain I never saw anything of Billy in the mornings. He had his duties to attend to. The idea of the Shahraban canal is this. Starting from the Diyalah River at Table Mountain, it runs down about fifteen miles, with little ditches built out at the sides to allow the water to run into each garden on the way. The Irrigation officer's work is to keep the levels and gauges right and see that the water is equally distributed according to the Arabs' gardens or crops. The barrages are mud-banks built up to prevent the water going to these gardens except in due turn, when it is let through to a certain level. But sometimes the Arabs bore holes in the barrage in order to get more water, and in consequence it is very difficult to carry water to the tail of the canal.

The time when I saw most of my husband was, of course, in the evenings, when his work was over. We would sometimes go across the river in a flat-bottom boat pulled by Arabs and ramble about what we knew as 'Cyrus's Palace.' This, I suppose, is the palace at Daskarah-al-Malik, mentioned by Mr. Guy Le Strange in his *Lands of the Eastern Caliphate*, where it is said that Daskarah 'appears to be identical with the celebrated Dastagird, where Khusraw Parwiz had his great palace, which history relates was plundered and burnt to the ground by Heraclius in *a. d.* 628.' The city itself, on the authority of old Mohammedan writers, was founded by Princess Gulban, daughter of the Chosroes dynasty.

I was unaware of its history, but was quite sure of the palace being there, caked over with mud and sand as it was, leaving very little to see. It was reputed to go deep underground and contain spacious halls, etc. Two gold lamps were supposed to have been found on the site during the war, but now it was all blocked in and no excavation allowed. I always used to think that I should find treasures, perhaps wonderful jewels that had been worn by some beautiful Persian princess; but my hopes were never realised. This further side of the river was very interesting. There were many shallow caves, which we were never tired of exploring.

On our side, where the huts were, stood the monument to the

14th Division, and just beside it 'Cyrus's Bath,' a big shallow tank which had originally been marble. On this side, too, there was plenty to explore. Enormous faces of Members of Parliament, disguised in Eastern head-dress, had been carved in the rocks by our soldiers during the war. Thousands of lizards lived in these rocks, and Billy grew quite proficient in throwing stones at them and hitting them, which made them hastily retire, leaving their tails behind them. I was merely stone-carrier on these occasions. The lizards moved far too quickly for me to get a shot anywhere near them. There were also chameleons to be seen, but, much as I wanted, I could never catch one.

Wrigley often came up to Table Mountain in the evening to play tennis. His old Ford was a wonderful 'bus,' considering its condition and the wear it had had. We used to hear it clattering along a great distance off; each journey I thought was its last, but it was still going strong up to August. The court was quite a good one, with a barricade of reeds bound tightly together at either end and stuck into the ground, to stop the balls. We would play a hard game until it was too dark to see, and then went back to the huts, got into our bathing-dresses, and off to the pool for a swim.

It was a splendid bathing-pool, banked on one side by Cyrus's Wall, from which jutted a springboard. At first I was very cowardly, as it was a common experience to tread on a tortoise, which I hated; but I soon got used to such details as that. Much worse was the plague of mosquitoes and sand-flies, which were like a mist over the surface of the water. One had to keep ducking completely to prevent oneself from being devoured by them.

We used to stay in the water until it was quite dark, when a lamp was brought to light us back to the huts.

We dined outside the huts, a little raised mud platform being made for the table. Inside it was far too hot, and the sand-flies too numerous. Table Mountain is noted for its sand-fly, if nothing else. Some evenings were appalling; in spite of every precaution I got horribly bitten. We had our beds put up on a hill near the huts, as if there were any breeze to be had it would be found there, and once one was in bed and the sand-fly net well tucked in one was more or less all right. There would only be a stray one to deal with, to which one could give one's whole attention!

As the temperature in the afternoons was at times as high as 126°, and our huts were only mud erections on the ground level, it was impossible to keep cool on land, so Billy had an awning put over the Ruz canal close to the huts, where there was a gulley and a tiny shingle-beach, also a rope stretched across, about six inches above the water; and after *tiffin* we used to get into bathing-suits and *topees*, then into the water we went. The current was so strong that after two steps in the canal we had to hold on to the rope tight, as it was impossible to keep our feet on the bottom and we were pulled straight out in the direction of the stream. This was great fun, and Billy taught me many 'stunts' on that rope. In midstream if you let go with one hand, it was a great strain to catch on with both again.

We could watch the wonderful coloured insects darting across the water. A kind of black butterfly predominated, but we only had to splash or throw a stone in among the rushes to stir up a mass of moving wings of all colours.

It was beautifully cool in the canal. In fact, at times we were obliged to come out and sit on 'the beach' to warm up; but by the time we had had a cigarette we were hot again and only too eager to get back into the water.

Sometimes, when we felt extra courageous, Billy, Wrigley, and I would swim the Ruz canal. Starting from the source, we could drop gently down a little way until we came to a bridge with two arches, through which the water rushed at a terrific speed, and after one had passed this there was nothing to stop one from being swept down by the stream.

We floated down sometimes between high barren rocks on either side, but always with rushes growing at the water's edge and big sea-thistles. I kept close to Billy all the time. He was a marvellously strong swimmer, and was always ready for any emergency. When at last we arrived at the rope by our beach we caught on to it and were swung under and up. It was all very exhilarating and made one feel very fit— though somewhat short of breath.

In July (I am anticipating a little) the *bund* was completed. Similar works had been constructed by the Arabs and by their predecessors for centuries, to hold up the water and to prevent it taking its natural course. The new *bund*, built by Arabs at the government expense, consisted of bundles of 'choke' thrown down one on the top of another and weighted down with shingle. The work had been commenced from both banks of the river, and the water thus grew deeper and swifter as the space between the two ends narrowed and made it necessary for the concluding operations to be quick and sure.

This building of the *bund* was a wonderful process to watch. Hun-

PREPARATIONS FOR BUILDING THE BUND AT TABLE MOUNTAIN

THE BUND IN COURSE OF CONSTRUCTION; AND MY HUSBAND
ON CYRUS'S WALL.

dreds of half-naked Arabs were running forward all the time, with bundles on their backs, throwing them down on the top of one another and stamping them down in such a way that it was very seldom that a bundle was washed away. Then at sundown an iron gong was sounded, and immediately there was a great cry of rejoicing that the day's toil was over (the Arab hates work). Each *sheikh* to whom the *bund* would prove beneficial supplied his quota of men. These *sheikhs* had reed huts on an island of shingle in the middle of the river, where they stayed to see that their men worked and the *bund* was finished as soon as possible—for, once it was started, there could be no delay.

When the work was completed there was great jubilation. At midnight the *coolies* filed off, on their way to their various homes, all singing together.

The days at Table Mountain were certainly never dull. At night, after we had gone to bed, there was something very mysterious about the place. Was it because there had been so much fighting in the neighbourhood and so many lives lost there? I often awoke and tried to imagine what it had all been like. Then the dreams I had there were so vivid and so lifelike. One I now remember particularly well. I dreamt that Billy and I were alone and attacked by Arabs in a place with high walls. At the critical moment my revolver missed fire—and I awoke. I could hear footsteps coming over the shingle where we slept, a most unusual thing in the solitude amidst which we dwelt. I quickly wakened Billy, who called out, 'Who is it?' Fortunately, it turned out to be merely an Arab who had, or said he had, lost his way. I never thought any more of that dream until I returned to England and saw a mention of it in one of my home letters. Then it seemed to me like a premonition of what was to come.

Other nights of more tangible anxiety I remember at Table Mountain. At one time a band of mounted robbers were busy firing at the head-works, or else could be heard shooting near enough to wake us up. When I asked Billy if it was safe, he always assured me that they were merely potting at jackals; but I was sufficiently alarmed to persuade him to have our beds moved down nearer to the huts. I felt sure that up on that hill as we were then, our mosquito curtains showing up distinctly, we were a very plain target for anyone.

When we returned to Shahraban after these excursions to Table Mountain, I could not help feeling rather shut in, with the town on one side of us and the gardens on the other. Compared with the openness of Table Mountain, Shahraban seemed close and confined.

Another charming place to which we used to go was Quizil Robat, a village about twenty-eight miles north of Shahraban. This was another stage on the great Khorassan (or old Persian) Road, leading out of Baghdad across the Persian frontier, and ultimately right up to the gates of Western China. It is said to have been a guardhouse on the road at the time of the Seljukian ruler, Malik Shah. Here we always went three together, Billy, Wrigley, and I, sometimes by train, at others in the car. The journey by train took us through the Jebel, amid glorious scenery on either side, with the Diyalah River winding in and out.

When we reached Quizil Robat Station (which we always did in the heat of the day) horses were waiting to meet us, and we had a ride of a mile and a half to the house of the Political officer of the place, a very fine billet. The first time I went no preparations had been made; but on following visits there were signs of much preparation. The big bedroom at one end was sumptuously arranged with Persian rugs, and the floors and side-walls were covered with them and bright-coloured mattresses and cushions. There was a large domed fireplace in blue, red, green, and gold in the room, and a beautiful Oriental ceiling with a design of coloured glass in the centre.

This house, which was one of the largest in the town and had belonged to a wealthy Persian family, was built in the Persian style. There was a small stone well in the front garden, with gulley-ways of stone to irrigate the garden. At the back was a small orchard, with a high mud wall all round.

On our visits to Quizil Robat, Billy always had to go out to see about the water, while Wrigley had official work to attend to at the billet. After *tiffin* (which was real Arab food and beautifully cooked), the men went back to their work and I was left to rest.

While I was waiting for Billy to return in the evening, I used to watch the innumerable bats that lived in the ceiling of the verandah outside the bedroom I occupied. There must have been thousands of them. They only had two outlets, about two inches long, and just wide enough for one or two at a time to get through. As the sun was setting, all of a sudden there would be a great squeaking and scratching in the ceiling, and the bats began to swarm out. Line after line they came, all scrambling to be first. They poured out like raindrops, and flew off for their evening meal. It is no exaggeration to say that they made a dark cloud above the verandah for fifteen minutes without ceasing until all were out and lost to view.

I loved going to Quizil Robat, especially when we went by road. This meant starting at 5 a.m., to avoid the heat, and arriving in time for breakfast. The drive was all through the Jebel, along the Persian Road, passing many caravans on the way, a wonderful sight in a wonderful setting.

CHAPTER 4

Summer Days

It was during one of our visits to Table Mountain that I was obliged to make a second journey to Baghdad. It was about the middle of June, during the Mohammedan Ramadan, which corresponds in a way to our Lent, when an unofficial wire came through to the overseer at Table Mountain, saying that a rising was expected in the Baqubah, Shahraban, and Diyalah districts, and that my husband must send me to Baghdad. Billy decided that I should go by the next train, which left at 6 a.m. in the morning. So I went with my Armenian maid, while Billy returned to his post at Shahraban. When we arrived at Baqubah, we were told that a captain and his wife—no one knew their names—had been shot in Baqubah Camp. This afterwards proved untrue. Nor was there any disturbance in Shahraban, except that a few of the Jews' shops were looted, and my apprehensions about my husband's danger were groundless.

When the new moon was seen, and the Arabs became normal, I returned to Shahraban. The stay in Baghdad had proved very pleasant, and it was good to talk with Englishwomen again. The journey back, however, was not so nice. I left Baghdad with my Armenian woman, in a truck. We had just passed Coningham's Post, and the train was getting up speed, when an Arab came running alongside and tried to jump into the truck. He could not quite manage it, as one hand was occupied in carrying his rifle. But he threw the rifle in and attempted to follow it. I shouted at him to go away, but he ignored me and finally managed to jump in. I promptly threw his rifle out, and to my great relief he jumped out after it.

When Billy met me at Shahraban, he said the man could only have been a *shahanah*,[1] and Captain Wrigley confirmed him, so really there

1. Arab district police.

had been no need at all for me to get in a panic; I was bound to laugh when I thought how I had kept the legs of the camp-bed near me to keep any other Arab out who tried to get into the truck. As for the Armenian woman, she had simply crouched down and covered her face with her hands.

I went again to Baghdad after another visit to Table Mountain. On this occasion it was because my horse took fright and threw me. I thought that my arm was broken in several places, and Billy decided to send me to Baghdad. First, however, I was fetched down to Shahraban the same evening. Captain Wrigley bringing his car up for me. The next morning we caught the first train to Baghdad, where he had himself to pay an official call. We started at 6 a.m., and I can remember how my arm hurt, and what a hopelessly long journey it seemed. It was 4 p.m. before we arrived, by which time my arm was much worse. But when it was X-rayed the next morning, nothing serious was found to be wrong, only a very bad sprain; Billy came over in a few days and fetched me back. So ended my last visit but one to Baghdad.

Back in Shahraban, I have no important incidents to record, and I can only jot down a few reminiscences as they occur to me. From a letter of mine written in July I see that I was sitting on the roof one night when I noticed in the distance, moving towards us, a dark mass. It reached from earth to sky, and seemed to be going at a rate of about eighty miles an hour. Everything was quickly removed from the roof, and the doors and shutters were closed; but we stood and watched for a while. It was really a wonderful sight, this 'sand devil.' At last it reached the edge of the gardens, and the tops of the date-palms were bent and the leaves all torn off. Fortunately, however, it passed on just outside the village and was lost to view.

Ordinary sand-storms were nothing, but I remember one terrific one. The wind simply howled, and everything about the house that could bang banged. The novelty of the thing made me go on to the roof to look at it. The storks had all gone off, except two baby ones in a nest on a wall nearby. They were struggling to get down into safety, but in vain, for the wind soon knocked them over and they were seen no more. I could not stop up long, for fear of being knocked over myself. But it was a great experience to see, through a cloud of myriads of sand-grains, everything in every garden bent in one direction, and the desert beyond looking dim and unreal.

Often at nights we could see a glow in the sky, and knew that somebody's crops were ablaze. Nobody seemed to worry about such things, and the next day one heard nothing about it.

I had a new pet presented to me by Captain Wrigley, a sweet baby gazelle, which loved me very much when Billy was out; but as soon as my husband came home I was nowhere, and it would only follow him about. Before his return, while I was expecting him, it would accompany me to the roof, and when I waved to him it would go down to meet him. In fact, as soon as 'Gazookah' (as I called it) saw any one on horseback, Arab or other, it would dash down and wait in the hall. Its calculations were often quite wrong, but I loved it for this little way.

Gazookah was exceptionally intelligent for a gazelle, I think; for they are not usually clever. It used to play together with Scut for hours. They would chase one another round and round the verandah, until at last Gazookah got tired of the game and ended up by trying to butt the dog.

At meal-times Gazookah was most faithful to Billy, standing with its chin on his knee, with an occasional shove to remind him that it was there, and would not leave him for the most tempting morsels I might offer it.

My poor gazelle's end was sad. About the beginning of August, I came down from the roof one morning and found it unable to stand. Its legs seemed paralysed. I sent for Fahal, whom I looked on quite as a vet., as he appeared to understand about all animals. He said that probably it had smelt soap or burning fat, and that if it were not better in two or three hours it would not live. The explanation seems strange; but, anyhow, Gazookah did not recover. When it died, we put it in the *khan* at the back of the billet, on a bed of grass. I went round later in the evening, and found nothing left but some tiny bones. The jackals had been there first!

Scut remained with me. We kept him at home as much as possible, as there appeared to be a great epidemic of rabies in Shahraban, and as one walked through the *bazaar* every dog looked in the first stages. Poor, mangy, uncared-for things, they slunk away, however, as one approached them.

Scut made great efforts to get out in the evenings and go round to mix with the Arabs in the coffee-shop. But his chief evening delight was to come on the roof and bark at the storks. He was very amusing then, always keeping at a respectful distance and making a furious noise. The storks persistently stood their ground, clacking with outstretched wings and making little dives at Scut, but I was always afraid that his eyes would be pecked out. Captain Wrigley's dogs, Girlie and Bint, were much more able to deal with the storks, dashing up on the roof and clearing them off in no time. There was only one they could not tackle, on their master's roof. This bird used to sit on a high pole, unmoved at the dogs' frantic barkings below it.

Sometimes we dined with notables of the town. I remember being taken to the women's quarters at one house, where a new baby had arrived only two days before. The mother was very young indeed, and was sitting up and smoking. The father seemed still younger. The baby was the weirdest little thing I have ever seen. Its face was painted and its eyes blackened, and it was wrapped tightly in swaddling bands. It was given to me to hold, and all the women, about twenty of them, gathered round and did their best to wake it up. But fortunately it did not cry, at least not while I was holding it. The cot was elaborately decorated with flounces and hangings of various colours, and a lighted lamp stood at the head and foot of it. It was all very interesting, but such an odour arose from that bevy of women that I was glad when it was time to go.

A date that I remember well was the 29th of July—the anniversary of our wedding-day. This was the last occasion on which we visited Quizil Robat, going with Wrigley in his car. The journey was a long one, with engine trouble on the way. We lunched with Captain Bradfield, whom we had met before. He was commandant of levies, usually stationed at Baqubah, but was now under canvas at Quizil Robat with fifty levies and their horses.

Early next morning we started back. We had some excitement on the way, as we managed to shoot a jackal, and saw many of the enormous long lizards which there are in this part of the country, and tried pot-shots at them.

August now arrived. . . . I see from a letter of mine, dated the 9th, that the Arabs in Shahraban were getting very 'uppish,' but we were not perturbed. It was true that a rumour was about that a notice had been posted up in Baqubah that all the white people were going to be wiped out, but we never met anyone who had seen the notice. As for Billy, he never told me anything that might alarm me, and so I had no expectation of evil to come.

STORK'S NESTS AT SHAHRABAN

CHAPTER 5

The Storm Begins

The first tidings which I had of the trouble north of Baghdad was on the 8th of August 1920, when I was sending my Armenian maid back to Baqubah Camp. She had a temperature, and I was afraid of malarial fever, with no doctor in Shahraban. I sent her in a bullock-cart, with cook to see her safely in the train. Cook returned alone, saying that the maid was staying at the station until the next train came through. No early train was running that morning, the line had been cut at Abu Jisrah, and there were wild tales of the station-master having been murdered, his throat cut from ear to ear, and of the whole staff of clerks having run away.

When Billy came back from his morning round of inspection, I was full of the news; but he said that the report was all untrue, and no one had been murdered. It appeared later that there had been an attack on the station at Abu Jisrah, but no one was killed, though the Baboo staff had run off and hidden in the ditches.

On the next day, the 9th of August, Captain Wrigley sent over a chit to say that he could not start his car. Would Billy go round and help, as the Arab driver had gone off to Baghdad without leave? When the chit arrived, Billy was still out. When he came back he went across to the A.P.O.'s, but found that part of the engine had been taken away by the driver, so that they could do nothing. They came back to our billet with Captain Bradfield, all very 'fed up' about the car.

It was now that I learnt that Captain Bradfield had come down from Quizil Robat, bringing with him the fifty Arab levies and their horses. The levies were stationed in the Qeshlah.

My first question was, 'Why, Captain Bradfield, we're not going to be attacked, are we?'

'Oh, they're always shifting us about,' he replied; and I thought no more about it.

They arranged to dine with us that night. Soon after they had arrived at our billet, a *shabanah* came to the house and asked to speak to the A. P.O. Captain Wrigley went down to see him. When he came up again to join us, he said that this *shabanah* had been attacked as he was coming through the Jebel, and his rifle and ammunition taken away from him. His face had been severely smashed about, and his ear badly cut, and he was very frightened.

I asked Captain Wrigley if anything was likely to happen at Shahraban.

'That's what I want to know,' he said.

'Haven't you asked H.Q. what you will have to do if anything does happen?' I went on.

'Yes, I have, and their answer is that it is most improbable anything will happen at Shahraban.'

In the course of the evening a chit, in code, arrived for Captain Wrigley, which he had to go back to his billet to decipher, as he kept the code locked up in his safe there and he had the key with him. Accordingly he and Captain Bradfield left us soon after dinner.

Billy and I sat on the roof talking for a long time after they had gone. His greatest worry was that he could not get me away. No trains were running—the last of them from Baghdad having stopped, as a matter of fact, on this same night of the 9th—and the car would not go. So there was no means of sending me off. However, Billy said, if any trouble were likely to arise, the first thing they would do would be to withdraw any women from the district; and he impressed on me that if a car was sent for me, and he was out at the time, I was not to wait for him to come back, but to go at once.

On the 10th the District Irrigation officer of Baqubah rang up, and Billy told me that he had said that a small raiding party had been shooting from the other side of the river at Baqubah; but it was nothing serious. Billy asked him whether he was sending his wife away to Baghdad. 'No,' the D.I.O. replied, 'it's only a little band, and they are just out after loot.'

When he came away from the telephone Billy told me there was nothing to be afraid of, and again assured me that if there were any likelihood of danger a car would be sent, which I must take without waiting for him. He naturally thought that a car would come. But, as will be seen, no car nor conveyance of any kind arrived, nor was any message or warning of danger sent through.

Of course I thought everything was safe and felt quite at rest—so much so that I set to work and made some toffee and sweets, the only things which cook could not make.

That evening one of the servants came up, very cross and indignant because in the *bazaar* they had refused to change a ten-*rupee* note, and would only take silver. At this my husband looked serious.

'I think, Zett,' he said, 'you are better out of this. I'll ring up and get the D.I.O. to send one of his cars first thing in the morning for you.'

He went to the telephone and tried to ring up Baqubah; but the wires were evidently cut. There was no reply.

Nothing of importance occurred on the morning of the 11th. I begged Billy not to go out for his usual ride of inspection, but he insisted on going. He explained that, if he let the Baboos see that he was alarmed, they would get the wind up. So he went and came back safely to *tiffin*.

After dinner a chit was brought over from Captain Wrigley, saying, 'Come round and sleep at the Qeshlah with your wife. It would be safer.'

We debated for a while whether we should go or not. Billy said that, if anything happened, the first place that the tribesmen would attack would be the Qeshlah. It was not for himself that he was troubled, but for me. He was strongly in favour of stopping in our billet.

I wanted to go to the Qeshlah. I felt that we should be safer all together.

We were still debating twenty minutes later when Captain Bradfield came round to the billet with six levies to fetch us. He talked for a time with my husband. Then Billy told me to get ready, as we were to go. He went into the next billet, where the Indian subordinates lived, and told them to be ready in ten minutes to come along with us to the Qeshlah.

Then I began to collect the things it was absolutely necessary to take. Those who are used to the luxury of electric light in every room can have little conception of what I had to do that night. It was a case of hunting about in the dark with only hurricane lamps to guide me. And all the time I was wondering whether there was any one waiting to shoot at us over the wall from the *khan!*

Nevertheless the work had to be done. I quickly changed into a grey frock, thinking that that colour would show up the least in the dark. All that we took with us were camp-beds, bedding, and lamps. Captain Bradfield told me not to take a suitcase, as we were only going to sleep the night at the Qeshlah, and we should be back early in the morning.

I went round to lock up the rooms, but could only find a padlock for the dining-room door. This worried me, as we were leaving two levies to look after the house, and I did not at all care for the idea of them going into my rooms. As it turned out, they only went and helped themselves to cigars, which they plainly did not like, as they tried several and left them unfinished.

It was a scene of great excitement when we were all ready and collected in the courtyard for the start to the Qeshlah. We were taking with us three Indians, cook, and our Armenian boy. We left behind the two levies and Fahal. I asked the latter to take our horses over to his own billet for the night; but he had only room for one, so took mine. The other, the army horse, was brought to our billet, the *syce* having gone off and left his charges to look after themselves.

At last we set off, Billy, Bradfield, and I going first, some levies behind us, then the others of our party, and the remaining levies bringing up the rear. There was no moon that night, but the starlight showed up everything clearly. I felt a bit frightened on the road, I must admit, as I expected at every bend and corner someone to dart out at us. The town, however, seemed absolutely deserted. No one was about, and even the coffee-shop near our billet was silent. The only sign of life was the pariah dogs, which growled at us as we passed. Our own pariah. Scut, accompanied us.

When we arrived at the Qeshlah we went in past the sentries at the gate and straight up to the roof, where Captain Wrigley was waiting for us. It was now about eleven o'clock, and we sat down and talked for a little. We discussed the situation. Billy was strongly for putting me in a *sheikh's* house until things should quieten down. Captain Wrigley, however, was very much against this suggestion, and said that I was far safer with them, as there was no Arab in Shahraban who could be absolutely trusted.

Our beds were now put up in a line, Billy's and mine a little apart from the others; and we lay down for the night. I do not think that any of us went to sleep. Billy told me that if any shooting started I was to roll off my bed and lie flat on the floor. This was a necessary precaution, the wall round the roof being only about a foot high and no real protection.

It was a wonderful night—moonless, but star-scattered, and the shooting stars were more numerous than I had ever seen before, not just one at intervals, but a continuous display the whole time. I lay awake talking to Billy for a long while, as we so often did. There was, indeed, much to talk about, and particularly our situation at the moment. One thing I was quite sure of, and that was that we could not be taken unawares. If any one were to come through the town the dogs would be certain to give us full warning. They had made enough noise when we came through.

The night passed without incident, and we were up early. At 4.30 a.m. Billy and I left the Qeshlah and walked back to our own billet. Here we found the two levies still sleeping, and Fahal prostrating himself in prayer in a corner on his praying-mat.

I sat on the verandah for a time, watching the various flights of birds which passed overhead. Whole colonies of different kinds flew by at intervals, sparrows being the laziest and last.

Cook went off to the *bazaar*. When he returned, he reported that very few shops were open. Evidently the townspeople also were in expectation of a visit from the tribesmen.

I wrote a lot of letters that morning, which never reached their destination. And so the morning went by.

At midday an aeroplane passed over, very high, which furnished great excitement, as it was the first that I had seen since I came to Shahraban. What it was doing I do not know.

In the evening the coffee-shop at the corner was quite deserted. Not a soul was there even at six o'clock, when it was usually crowded. This helped to confirm the impression made by cook's report earlier in the day.

Captain Wrigley had told us to come to the Qeshlah again that night. I felt that I did not mind this now. It even seemed rather exciting; and Billy said that it would only be for a few nights more, and then things would probably be all right again. There were some things to do, however, before we left. Billy spent a long time cleaning up his rifle and revolver. I had got a lot of padlocks from the *bazaar*, and so was able to lock up the rooms, putting all the silver and other valuables in the store-room, which had the strongest lock.

Then we set off again for the Qeshlah. Tomas, the young Arab *peon* in the office, asked Billy to let him have a rifle and stop the night in our billet. Billy consented, and gave him a rifle and a little ammunition, while I left my dog Scut in his charge. We trusted this boy thoroughly, with regard to both money and everything else, and he had always proved himself worthy of confidence so far. But it turned out afterwards that his object in asking for the rifle was merely that he might get hold of one for his own use.

We reached the Qeshlah without anything happening worthy of note, and passed the night there, leaving again early next morning. On our return we found everything all right.

It was now the 13th of August, and we arose little knowing what the day would bring forth. At 10.30 that morning Mohammed Din, an Indian overseer who was stationed at Table Mountain, arrived at our billet, saying that Table Mountain had been attacked by tribesmen during the night. When he arrived, only I was in. I saw that he had no turban on, having evidently run away just as he was when the attack came. His story was that the tribesmen had suddenly broken into his hut, but that he had managed to get away and hide in the rushes. His brother Ahmed Din was not so lucky. He was there with his Persian wife, from whom the tribesmen had demanded jewels. She had none to give them; then they set upon Ahmed Din, and wounded him. He succeeded in escaping, however, with his badly frightened wife, and they were now in a house some distance away and safe for the time. As for Mohammed Din, after hiding for the night, he had got away from Table Mountain and made for our billet.

He told me afterwards that he had previously been warned by villagers near Table Mountain to send away any rifle and ammunition he might have, as if he had arms his life would be in danger, but if unarmed he would be safe. He had accordingly sent his rifle and ammunition to our billet in advance the day before. Anything else he had left to be looted.

I was very relieved when Billy came back from his work. I had begged him not to go; but he had insisted, as he said he was not nervous.

'But supposing you were attacked,' I had argued.

'Then I'll show them what shooting is!'

He was not attacked. But he had hardly got back to the billet again when a terrific shouting and noise started in the street below. I looked out of the window and saw an amazing spectacle. Those who have seen—and heard—the ordinary bustle and turmoil of an Eastern *bazaar* could form but a dim picture of what was before me now. Men, women, donkeys, goats, and cattle were all pressing in one direction as fast as they could, away from the *bazaar*, jostling and stumbling against one another as they went. The men were heavily laden with their goods, or as much of them as they had not been able to pile upon the backs of struggling donkeys. Here and there a cigarette-seller with a large basket of cigarettes stopped to sell his wares, and then ran on with the crowd. The women, with their belongings tied up in bundles of striped cloth and balanced on their heads, were pushing harder than the men. One desire animated all, to get away as quickly as possible. Only across the road I could see an exception to the general rush. A woman in the house opposite was walking up and down in her court-yard, wringing her hands. Her husband had not yet returned home. His other wife was clutching her baby in a corner.

I ran downstairs and told Billy. He came up and looked out of the window, then turned to me and said that I must get ready to go to the Qeshlah at once. While he went next door to tell the Indians to come along with us, I prepared to start. But, really, I had no preparations to make this time. I did not wait for anything, but simply took my *topee*. Billy came back and fetched his rifle and revolver. He kept on telling me that it was all right, nothing to be afraid of, only the Arabs with the wind up, and did his best to put courage into me.

We all met outside the billet and started in the direction of the Qeshlah. When we got to the corner of the street we were met by a levy sent by Bradfield, who told us there was nothing wrong, merely a sudden panic among the townspeople. So we turned back. I was very relieved, as I had not at all relished the idea of going through the town that day.

When we got back to the billet, about 11 a.m., Wrigley came round and had a long talk with Billy. Then he asked me to get together all the stores I had, especially plenty of flour, as we might be besieged in the Qeshlah, and perhaps be there several days. There had been some firing near the town, he said, but no sign of the tribesmen as yet.

The servants set to work immediately, putting all our stores into boxes, and *coolies* carried them round to the Qeshlah. I packed up my most treasured things, jewellery, photos of my baby, etc., and got ready a small supply of clothes for Billy and myself, also not forgetting plenty of linen sheets, to use as bandages in case anyone was wounded. Next I had a last look round our billet—which I was never to see again like this—and put out an enormous supply of grain for the chickens. Then we went, leaving behind the two levies, the *peon*, and Fahal. The Indians refused to come with us, saying it would not be safe at the Qeshlah, and they were going to an Arab's house.

We walked across first to Captain Wrigley's billet, about 250 yards from the Qeshlah. This was a slow process, for on the way we encountered a number of Arabs hurrying away from the town driving their cattle. Where they were bound for I have no idea. I knew of no place of safety for which they might be making.

When we reached Captain Wrigley's billet he left us, to go back to the Qeshlah and assist in barricading it in readiness for a siege. Billy and I were left alone in the billet until about half-past twelve, when Bradfield and Wrigley came over. The latter said that he was going to send a message to Captain Lloyd at Deltawah. He sat down at once and wrote it out. As he finished, he said: 'If that doesn't bring help, nothing will.'

So it was as serious as that!

'Let me see, Wrigley,' I asked. But he had handed the message to the two other men and would not let me look at it. Of course he wished to avoid alarming me, but I think he made me realise our danger even more.

Just after the messenger had left, an Indian rushed in, all breathless and agitated, and cried that 'plenty' tribesmen had been seen galloping down from Table Mountain. He could not say how many—only 'plenty.' They were all mounted and riding hard, he said.

'Oh! let's get along to the Qeshlah at once,' I begged. But the men refused to get in a panic. 'We may just as well have *tiffin* first,' they said. 'It will be half an hour before they get here.'

I would much rather have gone without *tiffin*, and how I have wished since that I had been able to prevail on them not to wait! Who knows but what it might have altered the whole situation if we had gone to the Qeshlah earlier? However, they were not to be persuaded, and so we sat down to *tiffin* on a verandah outside. The men were all very quiet. In fact, there was hardly any talking done except by myself, and I am afraid I only succeeded in making myself a nuisance to the others. 'Do you think they will really come?' I kept asking. 'What shall we do if they do come? They surely won't try to get into the Qeshlah?'—and so on.

We had nearly finished *tiffin* when, all of a sudden, without the slightest warning firing started.

We got up at once and took our *topees*, while the men picked up their rifles. Then a levy rushed into the billet, shouting that the tribesmen were here and were galloping through the *bazaar*.

We ran down and out into the road, and immediately there was a sharp outburst of firing at close quarters. We had stopped too long at the billet! The tribesmen were on us!! I cannot estimate the distance exactly. It seemed horribly close—perhaps it was about 100 yards, perhaps more. There, on horseback, were about twenty tribesmen. We, of course, were on foot. Some eight levies were outside the A.P.O.'s, and as we turned in the direction of the Qeshlah, they formed round the door. I have an impression of two of the levies lying flat in the road. Whether it was to fire or not, I do not know. Anyhow, they had not been hit.

As soon as the tribesmen caught sight of us, they rode hard towards us and started firing afresh. I cannot understand why no one was killed, nor even struck. The levies fired in reply, but also without effect, for none of the tribesmen fell.

The three men were walking calmly in the direction of the Qeshlah, without the smallest visible sign of panic or agitation. Billy kept saying to me, 'Stay in front of us. It is all right. Just keep on ahead.' But I must confess that I was quite unnerved and lost my head completely. It was in vain that Billy and the others tried to make me calm. I ran from door to door along the street, knocking on them hard and calling for someone to open; but they were all fast locked. Then if I saw any niche I sheltered in it at once and refused to come out. And all the time I was crying to the tribesmen—who naturally could not hear—'Don't, don't.' Billy caught hold of my arm and tried to help me along, encouraging me all the time. The others, too, were telling me it would soon be all right; but I was too terrified to heed anyone.

I wish I could say that I took example by the bravery of the men; but I cannot. At the time I was absolutely panic-stricken, and nothing they could do would calm me.

The Qeshlah, as I have said already, was about 250 yards away from the A.P.O.'s billet. Half the distance was houses. The rest of the way there was on one side a low broken-down wall, on the other open fields dotted with scrub. When we reached this open part the tribesmen, for some reason, turned back and galloped off to the *bazaar*. Shots, however, continued to come from across the open fields, so that it was necessary to duck every now and again. I ran from scrub to scrub in search of shelter, hardly knowing what I did. The men occasionally turned and fired in the direction of the shots. As we got to the Qeshlah the bullets were whistling overhead. But we reached it without any casualties. I made a desperate rush for the last bit, and was in the building first.

INTERIOR OF THE A.P.O'S BILLET.

EXTERIOR OF THE A.P.O.'S BILLET (ON THE LEFT).

CHAPTER 6

The Siege of the Qeshlah

Before I begin the story of the siege, I may as well give a list of the little garrison which went through it. There were Captain Bradfield, Commandant of the Levies; Captain Wrigley, Assistant Political Officer of Shahraban; my husband, Assistant Irrigation officer of Shahraban; Sergeant-Major Newton; Sergeant-Inspector Nisbett; Mr. Baines (though I was not at first aware of his presence at the Qeshlah); myself; our Armenian boy Gosdan, and Cook; some Baboos of the political staffs; and fifty Arab levies.

This was the force—including non-combatants—on which it fell to defend the Qeshlah against the attack of the tribesmen. With regard to the latter's numbers, we had only seen some thirty in the street, but when I asked Captain Wrigley how many they were who were attacking us, he estimated them at between five and eight hundred. The odds, therefore, were not quite so overwhelmingly against us as the first reports of the affair made out. But, on the other hand, the native levies were new and untried—and, as will appear, their conduct was *not* what these same reports represented it to be.

We had with us at the Qeshlah a few Arab prisoners who had been sentenced for various offences. They were locked in a room at the back of the building, with a guard over them.

As soon as we had arrived safely at the Qeshlah, the gates were shut and bolted. I have mentioned that Captain Wrigley had gone over that morning to help to barricade them. There were only two doors to the building, gates at the front, and one in the stable-yard at the back. The gates in front were of iron bars. That at the back was of wood, and only had one wooden bolt upon it. Against it the Ford car had been pushed close up, as an extra security; but, apart from the bolts, this was all the barricading which it was possible to do.

Nevertheless, I somehow felt safe now that we had reached the Qeshlah, and thought it was all over and finished, and that we had won a great victory. I was so sure that if my husband was with me nothing could happen. Perhaps it was the reaction after that terrible journey through the street and the open road. When we got in, Billy took me to a little room which Captain Wrigley used as his office, and made me sit down upon a mattress on the floor. I could hear the bullets buzzing round outside. The heat was terrific.

I sat here until Billy came back a little later and took me to a large barn-like room at the back of the building, facing the yard where the horses were tethered, the windows of which had thin iron bars to them. This had been used by the sergeants as their living-room; its furniture comprised two camp-beds, a table, and a coffee-bench. There was one wooden door in the middle wall of the room. Bullets were occasionally coming in through the windows, so Billy put down a mattress on the floor for me. I lay down, suddenly feeling very tired. Billy and the two captains came in from time to time to reassure me and tell me not to be afraid—which at that time I was not.

At about 2.30—I could keep count of the time, for I had my wristwatch on me—Captain Wrigley came in, saying, 'My billet's gone west!'

'How do you know?' I asked.

'I've been watching the townspeople carrying my stuff away.'

Not long after, the three came in together and sat down to talk matters over. Things were not going well. The levies had been placed mostly in the front of the building, where they could shoot from behind the pillars of the verandah and from the low wall, and some on the roof. But half an hour ago two of them had deserted, and others had been running off in twos and threes since. Moreover, they could not be stopped from firing all the time and without taking aim. This was most important, as each levy was equipped with only 200 rounds of ammunition, while a reserve supply of 4000 rounds was taken, thus making 280 rounds for each levy, and it was essential that every shot should be made to tell. The levies, in fact, were quite out of hand, and would not obey their orders.

On the other hand, the shooting of the tribesmen at times was very good. Captain Bradfield had a star shot clean off his shoulder. Sergeant Nisbett's *topee* was knocked off by a bullet, and Mr. Raines's *topee* was pierced right through the crown.

Captain Bradfield was terribly worried about the deserters and about the growing shortage of ammunition. 'If only we had a couple of machine-guns!' he said. 'And I've asked for more ammunition, but it never arrived!'

About three o'clock our hopes were raised, only to be cruelly disappointed. An aeroplane was sighted, and the three officers came in for sheets to spread on the roof as distress-signals. I heard the machine coming, and went out into the yard to see it. It came straight over the Qeshlah, at a height of about 500 feet. It then turned and circled over our little fortress twice. The sheets were now on the roof, and the men were up there waving hard. Whoever were in the plane must have seen in what a plight we were, how few were the garrison and how many the tribesmen.

The plane turned away and went off. The men came down from the roof, however, full of hope. The signals had been seen, and the plane would come back, bringing Lewis guns and ammunition. If we could only hold out till they came!

The plane never returned. No Lewis guns or ammunition came to save us. What was the explanation? I have never been able to make out. Afterwards when I got to Baghdad I tried to find out; but all the answer I got was that I was too ill and must not worry about these things.

Now followed a lull in the firing. We thought that this was probably because the tribesmen had collected in the bazaar, out of sight of the Qeshlah, and were discussing the situation and the best method of attack.

Then the men came in and said that a strange Arab had somehow managed to get into the Qeshlah. Not knowing his face, Captain Bradfield had taken him for a spy and put him under arrest. It did not seem to me at the time that the tribesmen had any need of a spy, as they were well aware what our strength was. Tribesmen are not in the habit of tackling anything stronger than themselves. Still, the man may have been a spy. Anyhow, later he escaped, and with him went his guards.

About 3.45 the firing was renewed heavily from all quarters, especially from the neighbourhood of the gardens by the tennis-court, which was quite close to the Qeshlah.

So far, since my arrival here I had felt quite brave. But now something occurred to destroy my courage. I heard Sergeant Newton's voice on the roof calling out for a rope. The body of one of the levies was lying at his feet, and when the rope was thrown up to him he tied it round the body and let it down the wall into the yard. Try as I would, I could not help watching what was going on. As the body slid down, a trail of blood was left all down the wall. It was a sickening sight and thoroughly unnerved me. I think it was only at this moment that I fully realised that the tribesmen were out to kill all of us as soon as they got their chance.

At about 4.15 cook brought in tea, and Billy and the two captains came in. They were still quite calm, but had come to a decision to send an urgent message to Baqubah—not knowing, of course, that the day before Baqubah had been captured by the Arabs, with no British casualties.

As far as I can remember, the message ran something like this:

'Qeshlah heavily surrounded. Ammunition, water running short. If no help sent, propose getting away on horse 3 a.m. to Deltawah.'

The water question was a serious one, and the men were very troubled over it. There was only one well at the Qeshlah, and at this time of year it was not very full. As far as provisions were concerned, we had an abundant supply. But if the defence was to continue, water would be as great an anxiety as ammunition. There were the horses to water in addition to ourselves, it must be remembered.

The message was sent off immediately by an Arab on horseback; and now we thought for certain that help would come to us in the shape of either aeroplanes or light armoured cars. Then we discussed our plan of escape. It was arranged that at 3 a.m., if help had not arrived, we should leave with the remaining levies, and if necessary fight our way out through the tribesmen to Deltawah. This was indeed a forlorn hope. It seemed to me utterly desperate. But what was the alternative—to be reduced to surrender by lack of water and ammunition and end with a horrible death?

The three now went back to their posts and relieved the sergeants, who came in for tea. With Newton and Nisbett came Mr. Baines, commonly known as 'Sergeant Baines,' but as a matter of fact Assistant Grass Farm Manager of Shahraban. He lived in a house near our billet, but I did not happen to have seen him before this moment.

They did not stay long over their tea. As they left, I said to Sergeant Newton, who had been walking about on the roof, regardless of shots, as though the siege were an everyday occurrence: 'Sergeant Newton, do take care. You are asking for trouble on that roof. Do at least bend down as you cross, or I know you'll get hurt.'

He laughed. 'I've got a charmed life,' he answered. 'Don't worry,

I'm all right!'

He was always like this—brave, cheerful, and full of life, seeming to enjoy everything that came.

'But you have forgotten that today is Friday and the 13th,' I cried; for that thought had been running in my head.

They went out, and I lay down on the floor again. The firing was growing much stronger, and I felt thoroughly panic-stricken.

It was at this point Captain Bradfield thought it was advisable to make an attempt at terms. We could at least test the disposition of the enemy.

We did not take long to find out. Two of our levies were sent through the gates and along the road on the way to the *bazaar*, which the tribesmen had made their headquarters. With them they carried a piece of white material tied to a stick. There could be no doubt that we were ready to discuss matters with the tribesmen.

The two men were shot down.

After this Captain Wrigley burnt all the papers and paper money, locked up the chest of *rupees*, and threw the key down the well.

The firing still increased, and now the noise was terrific.

It was about a quarter to six when Billy came into the room and said: 'Zett, you must be very brave. The tribesmen are scaling the walls. The gates are down. We must put up as good a fight as we can.'

He turned to go.

'Oh! don't leave me alone,' I cried.

'I must go now, but I shall come back again.'

He went out. I took my suitcase, which had my jewellery and money in it, and I struggled to get the locks undone. I was in such a state that I fumbled in vain. One came undone, but the other resisted all my efforts. I had thought of taking the best pieces of jewellery out and putting them on, in the hopes of getting them away. It was the one small mercy Providence showed me in not letting me carry out my intention. I should probably have lost my hands for the sake of my rings.

Giving up my attempt on the suitcase, I pulled my mattress over into the corner of the room farthest from the door, and put two re-volvers—Billy's Colt and a little Browning—just underneath it, where they could be easily got at when they were wanted. We might indeed want them—very soon—to end it all.

The sound of firing was now continual, and mingled with it were the shouting of men and stamping of horses, a deafening noise. Then

Billy, Bradfield, and Wrigley all came hurriedly into the room together.

I looked at them.

'Where are your rifles?' I screamed.

Billy said one word: 'Gone!'

Very briefly they told me how, after they had fired their last shots, they had been surrounded and their arms snatched away. The levies had practically all deserted and given up their weapons without a struggle, only a few standing firm to the end. The few prisoners whom we had at the Qeshlah had been set free by the tribesmen. Nisbett had been shot at the gate. Newton was on the roof—they did not know that he had been killed. They had fought their way into the room, unarmed as they were, to gain a breathing-space for the final struggle.

What struck me then at the moment, as it does now with much greater force when I am able to think over the tragedy quietly, was the utmost calm and bravery that all the three men with me showed in this awful hour. It was this splendid behaviour of theirs which had led me to believe, up to the time when they told me of the loss of their rifles, that things were not looking quite so black.

But now what could I think? The end could not be far off.

A pathetic object, to add to our misery, was Captain Wrigley's black dog, Girlie, which followed her master about to the end. The last I saw of her was in a terrible state, all covered with mud and blood, as she wandered into the room looking for him.

Now that we were all together, and with us the Armenian boy and cook, we took up our position in the corner of the room farthest from the door, in two lines of three each. I was nearest the angle of the room, next me cook, and then Gosdan. In front of me stood Billy, then Bradfield, and then Wrigley.

We waited for what seemed like a minute, with an appalling din going on outside. Then Bradfield turned to Billy and said: 'I must try to stop this.'

He went out of the room, and we could hear his voice shouting in Arabic. Then came two distinct shots.

'Bradfield, Bradfield,' I screamed, 'come back!'

But there was no answer.

'I'll go out and see,' said Wrigley a moment later.

He went straight out.

I never saw either of them again alive.

The moment he had gone, a horde of tribesmen suddenly burst

CAPTAIN W. T. WRIGLEY, M.C.

into the room. Seen at close quarters, they were short-built men, dirty, and repulsive looking. Their *abbas* were tucked in at the belt to keep them out of the way. They were armed with curved knives, daggers, and rifles. The noise of shouting increased in volume.

They were firing aimlessly. The flashes from the rifles showed up in the growing dusk. The heat of the room was terrific.

Billy turned to me and said, 'Come on, Zett, we must finish it. Got my revolver?'

I had taken the revolvers from where I had put them, under the mattress. I handed Billy the Colt and kept the Browning myself. He told me what I already knew, that all the ammunition there was for the Colt was five rounds. There was plenty for the Browning; but it was little more than a toy.

'Don't fire until I tell you,' said Billy.

They were now right on us, surging around us. Some were busy looting, dragging out whatever they could lay hands upon, shouting, yelling, and quarrelling among themselves. The whites of their eyes gleamed horribly.

Then one Arab got sideways, and I felt him catch hold of me. He tried to pull me out of the corner. Then I screamed.

My husband fired—the Arab fell.

Then we put up a fight on our own in the failing light.

CHAPTER 7

To Sheikh Majid's House

I was out in the road, with a stinging pain in my side. In a dazed way I noticed a hole in the garden wall, through which I jumped, and ran on wildly across the garden until I came to a ditch. Then I lay down and hid, every nerve in my body throbbing.

I could not get my breath. My tongue was swollen, and my throat sore and dry from my continual screaming and the dust. I felt a mass of pain from head to foot.

The sound of firing was still going on. Presently I heard steps. Looking just over the edge of the ditch, I saw men coming towards me, hunting as they went in likely hiding-places; the first man was carrying a rifle. This was really the end, I thought. I stood up and called to them, trying to tell them where to shoot, and pointing frantically to my head and heart.

'*Yawash, yawash!*' (Gently, gently!) they said. So I knew that they were not going to kill me straight away, and at that moment I longed for death, my misery was so great.

They came up and took me by the arms and pulled me along. I tried in vain to pull back. I knew that Billy was lying dead, and I wanted them to fetch him too. They dragged me on. There were five of them in all, two of them awful-looking creatures in rags caked in dirt, the other three not quite so wild in appearance, but with most repulsive faces. They were obviously townspeople—had they been tribesmen they would have killed me then.

They brought me to a wall, which led to the roof of a *khan*, and this they made me climb with them. Here I had to sit down. Unutterably miserable in mind, and with every limb aching, it seemed another step was impossible. From sheer force of habit I looked at my watch, which had been overlooked by the looters in the Qeshlah. It had been too dark in that barn-like room to see so small a thing. My hands had been felt many times, to see if I had any jewellery; but my wedding ring was so small and their hands so hard and horny that they had not noticed it.

The time, I saw, was 6.40 p.m. Immediately my hand was caught hold of, and the men started shouting all together. A dagger was drawn, and a thrill of terror ran through me. I did not want to die that way. I wrenched my arm free and got the watch off my wrist as quickly as I could, and threw it in their midst, and they settled among themselves the question of its possession.

Then followed a discussion, in very heated tones, where they should take me. All said different names. The easiest name to catch, and the one most often repeated, was that of Sheikh Majid. I caught at this and kept repeating, 'To the house of Sheikh Majid!' Not that I knew him, nor had I the slightest notion who he was; but I was in mortal dread lest any of my captors should take me to his own house.

At last we proceeded. We went across the roof, down some little steps, and through the *khan* for a little. Next we climbed over another broken-down wall and came to the back door of a house.

A man knocked. A woman's voice answered. Then a man came, and after a little delay the door was opened. We crossed a courtyard, through another door, and into a second courtyard. It was almost too dark to see anything clearly. But a man came up and put a lamp near my face and looked at me. He pointed to the bloodstains all over my frock. A long conversation followed. What it was about I had not the remotest idea; but I suppose that the man with the lamp was surprised that an Englishwoman should be in such a state as I was in.

I was indeed in a terrible plight. My *topee* had gone, and my hair was half down. My frock was, curiously, not much torn, though my petticoat was torn badly; but it was spattered with bloodstains everywhere.

The second door was at length opened, and we stepped through on to the path by the canal, along which so often Billy and I had walked on our way to the tennis-court. What a ghastly mockery it all seemed!

When we came near the bridge, I could make out that a huge crowd of people was standing by it. As soon as I saw them, I began screaming again and tried to run back into the courtyard which we had just left. The men with me, however, prevented me and forced me on with them.

Then it dawned on me that the crowd was townspeople, not tribesmen. I pulled at the *abba* of the cleanest looking of my captors and made him take it off. I wrapped it round me, and after that I felt a little safer.

There was a great deal of murmuring as I passed through the crowd. They had obviously recognised me, in spite of the borrowed *abba*. But there was not a tribesman to be seen. All were still busy looting at the Qeshlah, I suppose.

The way led on to where our billet stood. It was now so dark that I could not make out much. But at least I could see that, as far as the outside was concerned, our old home was just as we had left it. The front door was open, it is true; but the curtains were still up at the windows, and the lamp had been lit in the entrance. Nobody appeared to be about.

We passed the billet, turned round the comer, and went down a narrow alley-way. This, I thought, could not lead to a *sheikh's* house, and I kept on repeating, 'This is not the way to Sheikh Majid's house; take me to Sheikh Majid's house!' But they made me understand that it was the way.

We arrived eventually at a door, at which they knocked. There was immediate silence within, until at last some one answered. This was the beginning of a long conversation through the door, of which I could not gather the purport.

All the while I went on saying, 'This is not Sheikh Majid's house.'

I still had, of course, no idea who the *sheikh* was, or where his house lay. And certainly, had I known of his identity, I should never have asked to be taken to him. As a matter of fact, as I afterwards learnt, he was a cousin of Sheikh Hamid, the head of those very tribesmen who had murdered our brave men. Apart from that, it will be seen that the house was an exceedingly poor one, and that the sheikh had not enough food to give even to his own women-folk.

Here I was, however, at Sheikh Majid's house, as I had begged to be brought. When the conversation had finished, a heavy wooden bolt was drawn back and the door opened a little way, then pulled wide open. I went through, followed by the others.

There was comparative quiet for a moment, and I looked round the sea of faces, all turned to the door through which we had entered.

I was, as may be imagined, in no state to take in details. There seemed about a hundred people there, perhaps more, all men. What stood out clearly to me above everything else was those cruel-looking curved daggers, of which nearly everyone had one stuck in his belt.

The courtyard into which we had come was a square, with rooms leading off all round. There was a mud floor, beaten very hard by the constant passing of feet. Benches were set in a square in the middle. On these some sat, while others stood about. The yard was lit by hurricane lamps, hanging on the wooden beams which supported the roof.

When I realised that the door was shut and bolted, and that I was locked in, I turned and pulled hard at the bolt, but could not move it. I screamed.

Then suddenly I heard, in English, 'It is all right, *Mem Sahib*, don't be afraid.'

When I looked I saw some of the Indian subordinates who had worked under my husband. There were about eight of them, and with them was Mohammed Din, who had brought us the first news from Table Mountain.

'Are they going to kill me?' was my first question.

'No, no,' said Mohammed Din, 'they will not.'

I would not believe him, and exclaimed to the Indians that I was going to be killed, and probably they also. 'But, Mohammed Din,' I asked him, 'tell them to shoot me when they come. Then it will be soonest over.'

He assured me again that they would not kill me yet. 'You are in their house now, under their protection, and safe for a while.'

This did not convince me. I had seen too much killing in the past hour to believe that I was safe, even for a time.

Now an old man approached, and I heard someone say, 'Sheikh Majid.'

I turned and drew him nearer a lamp, where I could see his face. 'Are you Sheikh Majid?' I asked.

I looked well at him. It was not a pleasing face which I saw. The eyes were small and watery, close together and very shifty, set in a rather long, sallow face, with a white beard. Immediately I felt that I could not trust him.

I stared at him for a long while. Then he suddenly began talking. I tried in vain to understand what he was saying; but he went much too fast for my very limited knowledge of Arabic to grasp his meaning.

At length an Arab boy, who could speak English, came up and began to interpret for me. What the *sheikh* said was to the effect that I must not be frightened. He would protect me. So long as I was in his house I need have no fear.

Well as this sounded, I was very far from comforted. I felt sure that the *sheikh's* protestations were false, that he did not mean them at all.

I made my first request, however. My *Sahib* had been killed, I said, and I must have his body brought to the house.

It was impossible, replied Sheikh Majid.

I begged him desperately to grant my prayer. It was my one desire at the moment, and I implored him to send someone to bring his body to me.

The sheikh repeated that it was impossible; and he appeared disgusted at the idea.

I turned to the Arab boy, and asked why I could not have my *Sahib's* body.

The boy shook his head. No, he said, it would be very bad. Sheikh Majid could not have him brought to the house.

It was useless to say more, and I was told that I was to be sent to the women's quarters. I was taken to a door, and passed through it out of the courtyard.

CHAPTER 8

The First Night in the Harem

I was in another courtyard. Women seemed to come to me from every quarter gesticulating and talking. They gathered round me and gazed.

I asked for water, which was brought to me. That was the longest and best drink that I have ever had, and the relief it brought to my parched mouth and throat is indescribable.

Now the women plied me with many questions, but all that I could answer was that my *Sahib* was killed. It was evident that they had not expected me, but they expressed their sympathy for me, striking their breasts with their hands and groaning.

They took me up some steep steps to the roof, and a mattress was brought for me and put down on the floor. The women sat round as closely as possible, all talking and making a great noise. They thoroughly inspected my bloodstained dress, fingering it and turning to one another, talking volubly all the while, and evidently in a state of great astonishment. They brought me a plate of rice which I could not eat. The mattress was very hard and painful, and I was glad when I saw a camp-bed being brought on to the roof. This was lent to me by one of the Indian prisoners, and I had cause to be very grateful to him for it.

I could not have rested on a hard Arab mattress that night, bruised all over as I was. I had but a hazy recollection at the time how I had come by so many bruises, only my face having escaped. But I recalled afterwards the horrible scene—the tribesmen striking at me with their fists and sticks. It was no wonder that I was black and blue. Why they did not touch me with their daggers I do not know.

It was quite dark on the roof, only a lamp affording illumination, but in the distance flames were now clearly visible on the edge of the town. I asked what they were, and was told that it was the Qeshlah burning. The tribesmen—with the help of the townspeople, as it subsequently appeared—having got all the loot out of it, set it on fire and destroyed it. This was the end of the Qeshlah, where so often I had gone after tennis to pick flowers to decorate our billet. Little had I ever dreamt that it would be the scene of an awful tragedy.

Later in the night the jackals howled louder than I had ever heard them before. Those who have heard their cry know what an uncanny sound it is, like the voice of a lost soul in distress. I always hated it when I was alone, and had never been able to rest, if Billy were out, until he came in. Then they might howl on the walls all night, and it would not affect me.

After a little I simply could not lie still and listen to this ghastly howling. I got up and began running about the roof distractedly, calling my husband's name again and again. The women started talking louder, and some of the men joined them on the roof, calling to me to stop. No one, however, attempted to prevent me from running on, and somehow it seemed to bring relief to my mind, in spite of the weariness of my body.

When at last I sat down on the bed. Sheikh Majid came and sat by, and talked a great deal. I only understood a few words; but as far as I could make out he was trying to say comforting things. When I prayed him, however, more earnestly than before to have my *Sahib's* body brought to his house, he absolutely declined. I argued that, if he would send a guard with me, I could carry him back. But he replied that I should be killed at once if I were to go out.

I thought at the time that it must be against their religion to bring the dead into their houses, but I learnt afterwards that this was not so.

The *sheikh* eventually left me, and a lamp was brought and put near my bedside. But I refused to have it near me, thinking that it would only be a good mark for anyone who might be waiting his chance with a rifle. Yet, all the while, I was hoping that if I was to be killed—and I knew that it was a sign of weakness in the Orient to show mercy—the manner of my death would be by shooting. A bullet would be quicker than a knife-thrust. I was torn between the desires for life and, if I were to die, a swift death.

Soon the women brought their mattresses up and lay down upon them, none of them going through the ceremony of undressing. Then there was quiet on the roof for a time. And now, how I wished that

THE QUESHLAH AT SHAHRABAN

they were up and making a noise again! While they had been talking, I had longed for peace. Now when it was comparatively silent I felt much worse. I could hear more distinctly the intermittent howls of the jackals, the cries of the mob in the town, and the sound of stray shots, some of which seemed quite close. I would have given anything for the women to wake up again and make a noise.

But there was nothing for me to do except lie upon my bed. It was a wonderful night, above the town. There was no moon, but myriads of stars were visible against the dome-shaped sky. Date-palms close at hand stood out, like tall spectres, in the radiance of the stars. There were not many mosquitoes about, although this night of the 13th August was one of the hottest of the whole summer. Two women came along the narrow path on the top of the wall that joined Sheikh Majid's to the neighbouring house, and sat down by a millstone to grind their barley for next day's bread.

About midnight the sound of grinding ceased, and all was still for a while. Suddenly I saw a man's figure arise on the wall which divided the women's roof from the men's, and stand silhouetted against the sky. I could discern a rifle slung across his back and a long curved sword at his side.

I gazed terrified, with my heart thumping hard. The man stood there for about three minutes without moving, looking towards the women's quarters. Then he jumped softly over on to our roof.

I sprang up immediately, screaming as hard as I could, and started running distractedly from side to side of the roof. At once a din arose, babies crying, dogs barking, and the women all shouting to one another. A lamp was brought, and a man came up to me. There was a great deal of talk and gesticulation, and I was given to understand that I had no reason to be frightened of him, as he was one of the household, and was only doing sentry-duty and seeing that all was right.

The man went away, and the women sat round me chattering vigorously for a long time. The burden of their talk was always the same, that there was no cause whatever for fear, that I was perfectly safe. But I could not bring myself to believe it.

When the babies had been got off to sleep again the women left me and went back to their mattress. I lay down once more and must eventually have fallen off to sleep, little as I wished to do so. But I must have slept, for early in the morning, before the sun arose, I woke up and found one of the women covering me over with a blanket. I was really touched at this, for she had awakened with the cold, and had got up and given me one of her blankets at the only time when they are needed in these Mesopotamian nights.

So ended the first night of my captivity.

CHAPTER 9

The Women's Quarters

The next morning, the 14th of August, most of the women went down into their courtyard before the sun was halfway across the roof. They left me in charge of two of their number, who sat in the shade of the wall and talked together. I pulled my camp-bed into the shadow cast by the date-palms which overhung from the garden, and lay there.

I had been longing for some tea ever since I awoke, and now I asked the two women if I could have some. One of them went downstairs, then came back and told me to go down. I went accordingly, and sat on the mud-floor with the rest of the women. There were no signs of any tea being made. After sitting till I ached all over, I asked for my camp-bed to be brought. When this was done I was a little more comfortable; but still no tea was forthcoming.

The Arab boy now entered who had acted as my interpreter the night before. As he comes considerably into the story, I may describe him here. His name was Hamid. He appeared to be at least nineteen years of age, but said that he was only sixteen. He had been to school in Baghdad, and spoke English fairly well. Besides being very good-looking, he was certainly the cleanest of those who came to Sheikh Majid's house. His long outer robe was always of silk and scrupulously neat. Like all the younger men and the boys, he had over his close-fitting skullcap a handkerchief of black and white check wound as a turban, the ends being tucked in, whereas the older men had the ends hanging down over their shoulders, just as one sees in old Biblical pictures.

Hamid was no connection of the *sheikh*, but he was constantly at his house throughout the day and sometimes at night. I fancy that his mother's home was in Shahraban, as he could always be found when

I asked for him.

He came now and sat down, saying that he brought a message from the *sheikh*; that I was not to fear and was to ask for what I wanted.

'Oh, Hamid,' I answered, 'he knows what I want, for my *Sahib's* body to be brought here!'

'No, sister, he cannot do that.'

'Why?'

'I do not know, sister.'

Hamid always called me 'sister'—the women said 'Madam'—and his great reply to questions was 'I do not know.' However, he asked me now if I would like some tea.

I had almost forgotten about tea for the moment, but said 'Yes' eagerly enough now. Hamid spoke to the women, and a hasty fire was made and a great show of preparation for my tea. The water was boiled and a teapot used in the same manner as in England. At last it was ready, and some tea was brought to me in a tiny glass, without milk but with plenty of sugar in it, and after the long anticipation I drank it eagerly.

Next I asked for water to wash with. They brought in a bowl and jug with a long spout. I washed in a most unsatisfactory way, as there was no soap to be found. The water was simply poured over my hands, after which there was a violent hunt for a towel. I was dry by the time it arrived; but I took it and kept it, as it was the only clean piece of stuff which I had seen so far and was therefore precious. The other women never made any attempt to wash during the whole time that I was in their quarters.

Then I wanted a brush and comb. My hair was in a terrible state, a handful having been pulled out the previous day among the tribesmen at the Qeshlah. A brush was not forthcoming, but a tiny bone comb was lent to me. The women all watched the progress of my makeshift toilet with great interest.

Finally, I asked Hamid for some hairpins, as I thought some might be fetched from my billet. But neither he nor the women seemed ever to have heard of such things, so that I had to get along as best as I could with my five.

At length I had time to look around the women's quarters or *harem*—though I never heard the word *harem* used in Mesopotamia. The name conveys to the average reader, I suppose, a picture of beautiful women sitting about on divans and brilliant-hued cushions upon a marble floor, amid gorgeous hangings, smoking languidly all the day through, while clouds of incense mount up from the braziers. What a different scene was that before me! The women were here—but far from beautiful—and the tobacco, but nothing else of the conventional picture, and certainly the perfume was not that of incense. The courtyard was a square of uneven mud, with dirt and filth all over it. In the centre was a horse-trough, also made of mud. Rooms, which might more properly be called hovels, led off all round the square. As one came through the door which led from the men's quarters and turned to the left, there was a mysterious room which was always kept locked. No one but Sheikh Majid ever went into this, except sometimes Sheikh Hassan, his son, in the company of his father. It was indeed a veritable 'Bluebeard's Chamber.'

Next came a room with only three walls, the fourth side being open to the air of the courtyard, where the chickens slept at night. Then another room which had in it only some old wooden boxes and some dirty discarded men's clothing thrown in a corner; and lastly, on this side of the yard adjoining the men's quarters, another empty room.

The greater part of the side wall next to this was taken up by a long barn, which was empty and never used, although it was the largest room of all. Two small room is followed, where cereals and straw were kept; and a rubbish heap intervened between these and the mud wall which divided the house from the garden. There was a well—dried up—by the side of this wall, and in the middle a little wooden gate leading to the garden.

On the outer side were more barns, in which they sometimes put the horses, and a little room where the barley and practically all the household goods and utensils were kept. And lastly came 'my room.' It was really everyone's room, but it was that in which I lived all through the daytime.

My room, then, was about 7 yards by 5, I should say. It had only three walls, the remaining side being open to the sun and air—and smoke, etc.—of the courtyard. It had at first no furniture except a low table against one wall, on which were stacked all the women's mattresses when they were brought down from the roof, and underneath which some rifles were hidden; and a baby's swing cot on a wooden frame, consisting of a cross-bar between two-legged supports at either end. My camp-bed was added to the furniture at such times as it was not on the roof. Oh, what a contrast this new room of mine was from the delightfully cool *surdabs* in our billet! Hot, stuffy, noisy, and dirty, it was always full of flies, which smothered the mud floors of the courtyard and pervaded everywhere.

From this room two steps led up to a door. Behind, in the angle of the courtyard, lay Sheikh Majid's own room, in which he slept during the afternoon, while his wife sat and fanned him, chanting some awful dirge, which was probably meant for a love-song. I never entered this room except once, and then neither my entrance nor my exit was a pleasant memory, as will be seen later.

In the extreme angle, behind the *sheikh's* room, were steps leading up to the roof of the women's quarters. This was like any ordinary Arab roof. There was a high wall on the side on which my room lay, at the back of which was a *khan*. A lower wall divided the women's quarters from the men's, and there was a staircase leading up from the latter to our roof. Another low wall was on the garden side, and the date-palms of which I have spoken overhung this from the garden. At the end of this a wall ran in continuation, with a narrow path at the fop, leading to our nearest neighbour's house. It was on this pathway that I heard the barley-grinders come the night before; and along it women would come in the evenings to have a chat with Sheikh Majid's womenfolk. The fourth side of the roof had no wall; there was a sheer drop to the courtyard below.

Now as to the inmates of these quarters. It is very hard to describe the women. After I became to some extent acquainted with them, the only one whom I did not dislike was Jumeila, Sheikh Majid's only daughter, who was aged apparently about thirty, or perhaps more. She was thin and had been, I should think, pretty. Her whole person was thoroughly neglected, and she had terribly bad eyes. Ophthalmia is painfully prevalent among the Mesopotamian women. In Jumeila's case one eye was completely bleared, the iris being covered with a white film, and it was constantly running with matter. This is horrible to write about. It was still more horrible to see.

In spite of this very unprepossessing condition, Jumeila was decidedly the best-natured and nicest of the women. Whether this was because she was the only unmarried one of the lot—'a maid,' as Hamid told me when he was pointing out to me the various women and recounting their histories—I cannot say. Most of the others might fitly be described as bad-tempered. Jumeila was not this. But then she had no husband to be jealous about, while the others had, and appeared always to resent them speaking to me. It seems that Sheikh Majid had never been able to find any man of whom he approved as a husband for his daughter, and consequently she remained 'a maid.'

Even Jumeila's good-nature did not extend very far. It was always she among the women whom I asked for anything that I wanted. She would assent and go as if to get it. But she would return without it, and when I asked again she would fail to understand my Arabic. I do not so much wonder at this, as I could speak very little, but I think she understood me, but pretended not to. She spoke no other language, but I noticed that she could read.

Sheikh Majid's wife, who was known by the name of Ummi (at any rate, it sounded like that), was rather fat, but had very good features and beautiful white hair, and her feet and ankles were shapely. She would, indeed, have been an elegant, handsome old lady, judged by our standards, if only she had washed. This she never did, and the before-mentioned feet and ankles were quite spoilt by their complete neglect.

Ummi had a whining voice, and was totally blind. I avoided her as much as possible, for whenever she sat near me she tried to discover what I was like by feeling my face. I really could not put up with this, for her hands were indescribably dirty. She paid me the one and only compliment which I received there. At least, I suppose that it was meant as a compliment, though I could not feel sure of Hamid's interpretation. According to him, Ummi said that I had a 'clever voice'!

Ummi had a sister living in the house, younger than herself, but a very plain woman with no likeness to her.

Then there was Keremah, whom I first took to be Jumeila's sister, as they were somewhat alike in appearance. It turned out that she was not her sister but her sister-in-law, being the wife of Sheikh Hassan. She tolerated me at the beginning, but obviously did not like me later. No doubt the fact that Sheikh Hassan would occasionally come and speak to me was responsible for this, little as I could help it.

Keremah was thin, but she was very graceful, with large brown eyes. She had three children, two boys and a girl. The elder boy, Huzain, who was about eight, was the cruellest child to animals, that I have ever known. He was continually bringing back birds from the garden and teasing and torturing them till they were so injured that they could not fly. Then he would toss them away. I only once tried to take one away from him. He called his mother, who came and abused me angrily, after which I never again attempted to interfere with anything. The other boy was a baby of nine months old, who was a great source of joy to the whole household. Ummi was devoted to him,

70

and was continually sitting and rocking him. The daughter came in between the two boys (I cannot remember her exact name, but it was something like Leg-Leg, which I called her). She was a bewitching little thing. Always happy and chatting, running about the courtyard, her anklets studded with bells all round told of her comings and goings.

Both the *sheikhs* had but one wife each. Some of the relatives, however, indulged in more. Legally a Mohammedan may have four, but the Shiah sect (which prevails in Mesopotamia) also allows additional temporary marriages. A man's financial position is naturally a restraining influence in such a matter.

The most painful object among the women was an old widow named Barkah, who was some sort of connection of the family, I do not know what. She was the mother of a particularly objectionable man called Mohamed, who had two new wives from Baghdad and lived in an adjoining house, where they had a proper bed and real mosquito curtains, as could be seen from our roof. Mohamed was a haughty-looking man, always covered with weapons, and he had a horrible habit of slouching in and out of my room as if it were his own, eating dates and spitting the stones out on the floor. Barkah's age appeared to be between seventy and eighty, and she was thinner than any one I have ever seen—in fact, a mere framework of bones, with loose dried-up skin covering them. Her eyes were sunken in her head, and her mouth was toothless.

Hamid said that she was dying because she was 'too old.' But it was clear that she had some terrible malady and was in continual pain. At times she would roll on the floor, and she was constantly moaning. The callousness of the other women towards her was dreadful, especially of one who was also the widow of the same late husband. But it must be admitted that there was little wonder that they avoided her company. The appalling odour that arose from her was overwhelming at close quarters. I too was obliged to avoid her, and, much as I pitied her pathetic state, I found her unending moans a fearful infliction,

A contrast to the poor Barkah was Sonieh, who was decidedly the prettiest of all the women I saw. She had wonderful brown eyes and masses of *henna* stained hair. She alone of the women was clean and took an interest in her appearance. According to herself, she was twenty-three, but I don't think she could have been more than nineteen. She was a cousin of Jumeila, and was in the house nearly all day long, going back in the evening to sleep at her father's, which was just opposite.

Sonieh was the *belle* of Shahraban, and was very willing to be married, I should say. It appeared that her father had not suggested such a thing to her as yet, and, whether he thought she wanted a husband or not, he would take no steps to find her one, so she had nothing to do but wait and hope for the best! She was extremely particular about covering up her face whenever a man came near. It always struck me that the ugly ones among these women were only too anxious for their faces to be seen, while the younger and prettier ones were very coy. Sonieh seemed all of a flutter on the approach of a man.

There were four other women who lived in the house. They always sat together on the opposite side of the courtyard from the rest and talked among themselves. They did no work, but smoked a great deal. They seemed to have no menfolk of their own, and they were never spoken to unnecessarily by the other women. At night they slept apart on a different portion of the roof from the others. To the end they remained a bit of a mystery to me, and I could never get to hear anything more about them than that they were relatives staying in the house. But any way they were quite harmless. They spoke to me very little, and would only occasionally let their curiosity go so far as to touch my clothes.

As for the women's own clothes, all in the house wore long flowing dresses down to their feet, cut on a yoke, and with a wide frill round the bottom of the skirt. These dresses were made of printed cotton material, mostly with a design of red flowers against a white background. They had black silk handkerchiefs doubled three-cornerwise, worn low over their forehead, crossed at the back and tied in a knot on one side. Over all was an *abba* covering the head and falling right to the ground. The women's *abbas* were always black, but were sometimes ornamented with gold braid round the head-part.

I have mentioned now all the women who (except Sonieh) actually slept in the house. But, apart from these, there were very many others who spent nearly all their day there and only went home at night. They did not belong to the household, but were obviously on most intimate terms with it.

It would be extremely difficult to give an idea of how the women spent their days, apart from what will appear in the course of my narrative. Their life was hopelessly monotonous. They rose very early, about 5.30. Jumeila and Keremah did practically all the work that was done—and that was very little. 'Tidying-up' was a rare event, as when some important visitor was expected, and the place was never swept except when it was absolutely necessary to do so. The getting of food for themselves seemed a very minor detail with the women, and barley-bread was their staple food. They lived and chattered and smoked amid dirt and squalor. Their only relaxation was quarrelling. As for sanitation (a most important matter for Europeans living in the east), the state of affairs was horrible.

I do not think I can be accused of exaggerating when I spoke of the difference between the quarters in which I found myself and the conventional picture of the Eastern *harem*.

CHAPTER 10

Some Visits and a Surprise

During the whole of my first day at Sheikh Majid's house my wounded side pained me terribly. I longed to get somewhere alone, to examine it, but the women would not leave me by myself for a moment, so I had to bear the pain. Other women came in, in numbers, from neighbouring houses, to gratify their curiosity. They all sat down and stared at me for a long time, and talked about me to each other. In normal times I am sure that this would have embarrassed me. But I now felt that I did not care.

For my midday meal I was given a piece of watermelon and some Arab bread. I had not often tasted this bread before, and I did not like it at all, nor did it agree with me. But hunger at the moment did not trouble me, and all that I felt I wanted was water.

Besides the women visitors there were a few men. Visits from the men's quarters were a source of terror to me. Every time that any one came in from their quarters to ours the door creaked, and I would jump up in a panic, thinking that it was someone coming to kill me. I could not get used to the sound of that horrible door. Nor was my alarm so unnatural. It was certainly not reassuring to keep hearing stray shots from time to time outside. They told me it was only the townspeople practising with new rifles. This was no doubt true. They had looted plenty of them in the Qeshlah.

Sheikh Majid did not come near me all day. Hassan, Keremah's husband, came in two or three times, always seeming in a hurry. He was very unlike his father, of medium build, very dark, with projecting teeth, and rather dirty-looking.

Another man I saw was Jassim, who appeared to be a sort of retainer of the *sheikh*. Anyhow, whatever his capacity, he was evidently one of the household. He was a big, dark man, always dressed in a dirty butcher-blue overall, which he never changed, the only alteration he made in his attire being the belt. At first I was frightened of him, as he always carried so many arms about his person, but afterwards I came to like him better than the others. He at least would generally lay his rifle down when he came near me, whereas the rest carried theirs in a most alarming way, pointing in my direction.

(Practically all the men, I may say, that I ever saw were most heavily armed except Sheikh Majid. They had *bandoliers*, daggers in their belts, often long curved swords, rifles slung across their backs or in their hands—a perfect armoury of weapons. The *sheikh* never appeared to be armed; but I found that the stick which he always carried with him was really a sword-stick.)

Then there was a very old man, who used to make the coffee, and another man, who carried in the water from the canal—for the well in the courtyard was dry. This last man was of loathsome appearance, and absolutely filthy. Directly I saw him I remembered his face. I knew that I had seen it once before at the Qeshlah. When he noticed me looking at him, he glared at me and turned his face away. After that I tried not to let him know that I had recognised him; but I knew that he was one of the townspeople who had joined the tribesmen in the looting.

These men and the boy Hamid were the only males who came freely into the women's quarters. There were, of course, the children. The little boy Huzain appeared that day with his pockets overflowing with coloured embroidery silks, which I at once recognised as mine. I had been doing some embroidery in my billet, and had left the silks in my *surdab*. I knew that at any rate the padlock on the *surdab* had been broken. Had, then, the billet been looted? But at this moment Huzain's mother came and spoke to him, and then sent him away. No doubt she hoped that I had not noticed the silks, which I pretended I had not.

I asked Jumeila, however, if it would be possible for me to get some clean clothes from the billet. She gave me to understand that when Sheikh Majid returned he would see that some were got for me. This was the first time that I made this request. I repeated it hundreds of times, without effect. How it was finally answered will be seen later.

Hamid paid me another visit, and I screwed my courage up to ask him details about the Qeshlah. Had all been killed? 'Everybody killed, sister,' was his reply.

Of course, I already knew the worst about some of our gallant party. As long as I live, the vivid memory of stepping across Captain Bradfield's body as I ran out of the Qeshlah will never leave me. But I was not up to now quite certain about Captain Wrigley. Hamid, however, asserted that all were killed, not only the British, but even cook and the Armenian boy. The last two had their throats cut—'very wide,' he said, with ghastly emphasis drawing his finger across his throat from ear to ear.

It gave me a pang as I thought of the two servants, especially poor Gosdan, whom I remembered quite recently rating for stumbling on the stairs with a tray of glasses and smashing them. I recalled his talk of his mother 'with the blind eyes,' and wished I had not been so severe.

As for the others, the British, I had had little doubt that all had perished. Yet the confirmation of my fears was none the less awful. All were gone, and here was I still alive. Why was I left? It was not my wish, and I did not care how soon I went to join them.

'When shall I be killed?' I asked Hamid. I wonder how many times I had asked him that question.

He made his usual answer, 'I don't know, sister.' He did not, like the others, hasten to assure me that I was quite safe. But as I did not care, so long as it was a quick death, his answer had little effect on me.

The day seemed to pass terribly slowly. I felt very much the absence of my wristwatch. A small consolation amid the general monotony was that I could have Arab cigarettes. These were homemade, of pure tobacco, rolled up in long papers bought in the *bazaar* and turned in at the end to keep the tobacco from falling out. They were rolled in such a way that the end which one put in the mouth was smaller than the other. They were considerably stronger than our ordinary cigarettes, and I could not smoke many without making my throat sore.

The women never left me alone, but I cannot say that their company lessened the monotony. They did not cease talking for a second. While Hamid was with me they could not understand my English conversation with him, but they continually questioned him as to what I had said.

When the shadows began to slant in the courtyard I asked if I could have a bath. This set them all chattering harder than ever. There was a terrific talk and fuss about getting it. A round tin tub was at length brought for my inspection and put in my room. I made them understand that I could not possibly have it there, with every one passing backward and forward. So they took it into the empty room which I have mentioned before, next to the chicken's night-quarters.

Water was poured into the bath, and a kerosene-tin of more water was set at the side, with a little bowl floating on the top, to be used for rinsing purposes. But where was the soap? More great fuss and excitement followed before some could be found, and when it arrived it turned out to be a bar of Sunlight. I still had the towel which had been given me in the morning; and a flannel was provided, which was a fine sort of loofah.

When all was ready, I asked to be left alone. The women sat down solidly, however, and refused to go. I sat down, too, intending not to have the bath until they had gone. But it became evident that they were determined to stay, and at last I had to make up my mind to bathe with an audience. It was an embarrassing task. They took great interest, and expressed much surprise that I was not tattooed as all of them were.

I found my side terribly inflamed and swollen. I knew that there must be some shot in the wound. I asked if I could have a doctor. Yes, they said, one should come the next day. There was nothing I could do that night, so I finished my bath and dressed again. It was most uncomfortable having no clean clothes to change into, nor even anything to put on while my present clothes were washed; but when I asked Jumeila she simply answered that they had no clothes to lend me.

After the bath I went up to the roof to lie down. I was beginning to feel hungry. I had had nothing since the meagre midday meal, and the cigarettes, welcome as they had been, had not entirely stayed my hunger. I asked for some food, and some boiled rice was brought me, very plain and uninteresting, but at least filling for the time!

That night was uneventful.

On the following morning it was obvious that the news that I was in Sheikh Majid's house had spread through the town quickly, as even before I was up a number of women came up to our roof and stood around me, staring and chattering. It was almost unbearable and made me feel a mere bundle of nerves. The noise they made would have given me a headache in ordinary times; but now, after all I had gone through in the last two days, it drove me frantic. I sat up, whereon, immediately there was room, women sat down on the bed on either side of me, fingering my clothes and hair and putting me through a most thorough inspection. Then they wanted to have a look at my teeth, which I stubbornly resisted. The last straw, however, was when one of them caught hold of my ankle and commenced to appraise my leg.

I could stand it no longer. I pushed her away and told them all to go. I sat on the bed, tucked my feet under me, and began to cry hard. It is a curious thing that not at the most intense moments of our lives do tears come, but afterwards, when the reaction has set in, and then a mere triviality will start them. Now I could not stop.

The women called to Jumeila, who came up and told me not to cry. She gave me a cigarette, which I did not want. Then she began to cry, too, and that set them all off. How they could summon up tears thus at a moment's notice I do not know; but there they all were, weeping and moaning and apparently displaying the most genuine sorrow.

I grew annoyed. I tried to explain that they had not known my *Sahib*; if they had, they would never have allowed this to happen. They could not understand a word I said, but they continued their lamentations, gradually gathering strength in their wails. To crown all, Keremah's baby was crying now. At last Jumeila told me I had better go downstairs. My bed was taken and put in my little room. The women came down with me, but they had ceased crying by this time and left my tears without accompaniment .

I was desperately longing to be left alone. This was the last thing, however, which they would dream of allowing. Nor could I escape from them anywhere, for it would have been madness to sit in the courtyard without a *topee* to protect me from the sun. More women kept on coming in, making me jump up in a fright each time any one arrived, until the floor was absolutely littered with them and their babies. They all sat round me, smoking and spitting and chattering. The whole place buzzed—and not only with women, but with flies. I asked for something to keep the latter off, and a long piece of muslin was unearthed and washed and lent to me. This was a great boon, for it did at least serve its purpose. I lay down on the bed, pulling the muslin over me, hotter though it made me, and waited till the women should go. At last they began to straggle off, and left me in comparative peace for a while.

Then Hamid came in through the creaking door, with Sheikh Hassan. Hamid talked to me, while the *sheikh* stood by. He made ordinary conversation at first, and politely brought me a pitcher of fresh water and put it by me. Then he began asking me a lot of questions. What nationality was I? 'English,' I answered (I afterwards wished I had said 'American'!)

Was I a Jew? he continued. 'No, certainly not'; but I wondered

78

whether I had done wisely in disclaiming this so promptly, and asked him what religion Sheikh Majid was. 'Mohammedan,' he said, 'and we do not like the Jews—they are no good.'

I was relieved. For all I knew, I might have made a mistake. There were a great many Jews in Shahraban.

'What is the ring on your finger?' was the next inquiry. 'Is it gold?'

'No, it is only brass,' I lied. 'All English women wear brass rings on their fingers to show they are married.'

'Show it to us,' said Hassan. But I declined, protesting that it was very bad luck to take it off. He did not insist, however.

Hassan and Hamid talked together for a little and then went away, appearing quite satisfied.

The women of the house, I noticed, were very happy on this particular day. Everyone appeared to have plenty of *rupees*. Neighbours, too, came across the roof, calling to one another and jingling money in their hands. They compared amounts, a process which ended in quarrels, not violent ones, but with voices raised very high, nevertheless.

Another curious thing which I noticed that afternoon was, that two coolies came into the courtyard bringing a huge Arab trunk, all bright colours like a patchwork quilt, and studded at the joins with brass nails. Sheikhs Majid and Hassan followed, and when the *coolies* had deposited the trunk outside the mysterious locked room, the *sheikhs* unlocked the door and took it in alone. They remained there some time, and when they came out locked the door again and tested the padlock. Before they went they came over and looked at me; but I had my eyes shut and the muslin right over my head, and to all appearances was asleep.

I had little doubt that within that trunk were many things from my billet; and as for the *rupees* which all the women had been jingling, they were doubtless loot also.

I was left practically alone for a while. Then came a great surprise. Hamid returned to see me and told me that the 'Sergeant of the Grass Farm' was at the house.

I jumped up.

'But you said that he was dead!' I cried.

'Not quite, sister,' he replied. 'He was brought here with plenty wounds, very bad, but not dead yet.'

Baines alive! An Englishman still living in the same town, in the same house as myself! It was a tremendous shock, but a very welcome one, as may be imagined.

'Could I see him?'

'Yes,' said Hamid, I could come into the men's quarters and speak to him.

I followed Hamid through the door which divided the men's quarters from ours.

Chapter 11

Another Survivor

I went into the men's courtyard, in which I had only been before on that night of 13th August when first I had been brought to Sheikh Majid's house. The arrangement of the yard was much the same as the women's quarters, with stables and rooms leading off it and a roof covering part of it. In a room corresponding to mine, but larger, lying upon a hard mattress on the floor, was Baines.

Poor man, he looked in an awful plight. His shirt was torn and smothered in dry blood. Both his arms were bandaged, in anything but clean rags. The Indian subordinates whom I had previously seen were sitting round him on the floor.

I knelt down beside him.

'Were you the last to leave the Qeshlah?' I questioned eagerly. The conversation went on something like this.

'Yes, I was lying unconscious among the shrubs when the Qeshlah was set on fire. When my clothes began to smoulder I came to, and some townspeople got me out and brought me here.'

'Did you see my *Sahib's* body?'

'No.'

'Are you sure you didn't?'

'No, I did not see him.'

I could speak no more. Utterly overcome, my one idea was to get back to my own quarters. Even though I was in such agony of mind, I must not let myself break down before all those Indians, so got up and went away. Only a few minutes before, the news that a fellow-countryman was close at hand had cheered me up tremendously. I had known, of course, that the Indian prisoners were there; but had attached little importance to their neighbourhood. Directly I had heard that an Enghshman was here, safety seemed already nearer. But at the sight of Baines lying there, so badly wounded and helpless, all the horror and tragedy of the last few days surged over me; and though I tried to gain control over myself, I knew that directly I attempted to speak again I should break down. So I was even denied the solace of a few more words with a fellow-countryman. It was evident that he would be quite incapable of coming to my assistance in case of need. We women cannot help such selfish thoughts arising at a time like this. When I was out of the men's quarters I could not keep back my tears.

The women were all back in their courtyard when I returned, and preparations were going on for the evening meal. Jumeila spoke to me and told me not to cry so much. This only had the result of increasing my tears. She brought me some tea, and told Hamid to say to me that it was foolish to cry like this. My *Sahib* was dead, and tears would not bring him back to me.

'Oh, Jumeila, I wish that I was dead too,' was all I could answer. 'Why didn't they kill me too?' I turned to both Jumeila and Hamid.

'I don't know, sister,' was the only consolation I got from the latter. And what was the use of talking to them? They could not understand. I said no more, and sank back into my own thoughts, desperately asking myself why I had run and hidden in the garden instead of waiting for death to come and take me to Billy. I should then have been with him now.

I was interrupted from my sorrow by the arrival of 'the doctor.' This proved to be a filthy-looking Arab, with a repulsive, leering face. He carried with him a jamjar containing stuff that looked like Mobile oil, and had a dirty penknife stuck in it.

I took one look at him and said, 'No, I didn't want a man, but a woman-doctor.' A long argument followed between him and Hamid, at the end of which I was told that a woman-doctor should be sent for. Of course none ever came. There was not such a person in the town. As it turned out, however, in a few days my side grew better without a doctor's assistance, and one evening, after my bath, I got out of the wound a little black ball, like buckshot. Then the swelling went down—and how thankful I was that I had not allowed that doctor to attend to me! Undoubtedly I should have got blood-poisoning if I had allowed him to use that dirty knife on me.

This same evening that I had visited Baines I asked for a bath. I say 'asked,' but when Hamid was not there most of my requests were made by signs. The women seemed very astonished. As they took no baths, it was doubtless a very strange thing for a woman to have two on successive days! However, one was prepared for me. The same scene occurred again which I had been through before. They gave no indication of leaving me. It was in vain that I protested. They simply declined to go, and I had to give way as before. During the whole time that I was at Sheikh Majid's, I never had a bath without the women being in the room. I could not get used to it, and in consequence my baths were always very hurried until I got to the petticoat stage.

On this evening my audience all took a great interest in my bruises, which were now in the stage when they showed very badly.

As for completing my toilet properly, that was perfectly impossible. I had, of course, no toothbrush, and knew it was useless to ask for one—and indeed I never saw one used. I managed fairly well, however, with the corner of my towel.

I asked for some clean clothes, but with the usual result. I explained that I knew that there were plenty in the billet. This had not the slightest result. Then I begged for some cold cream, just one pot, to be fetched from my bedroom. The heat and my continual tears combined with the Sunlight soap had had such an effect on my skin in the last two days that it was most horribly dry, and my lips were so sore and swollen that they hurt with each intake of breath. But no cold cream was forthcoming.

After I had finished my washing and dressing I received a visit from our former *peon*, Tomas, whom I had not seen since we left him at the billet. He spoke a little English, and I had some talk with him. I asked him whether my *Sahib* had been buried. 'Yes,' said Tomas, he had. He himself had helped to bury all. Everyone had been put into a common grave in the graveyard near the Qeshlah. After further questions, he explained that on the morning following the capture of the Qeshlah a hole had been dug, and the dead were laid on their sides, just as they were. The *Sahibs* had their watches taken away and any little things of value, and their shoes; but that was all.

The *peon* said that he was sure of this. However, the same evening Fahal came, and he had a totally different story. First he told Hamid to tell me not to ask him any questions. Then he started weeping; but, with a woman's persistency, I made him talk. When he had given his version. Sheikh Majid entered and sent both Fahal and Tomas away, after he had questioned them. Then he sat down and spoke to Hamid. According to what Hamid repeated, what really happened was that my *Sahib* and the others had been washed and wrapped in clean linen and all the English buried together.

This I knew was not true. I knew, or at least thought at the time, that the *peon's* account was the true one. Since then I have heard so many different tales—all from eye-witnesses, so they said—that I cannot decide what to believe. And, after all, what did it matter to the dead, so long as their end was quick and unexpected? It was certainly quick. As for unexpected, I wonder! It is difficult for me to understand how death could have been faced so fearlessly as it was by our little band of British if they had been expecting it. But I think now they were trying to keep the knowledge of our peril from me as long as they possibly could.

★★★★★★

There was a large party held on the women's roof that night after I was in bed. (I say 'in bed'; but all that this means is that I took off my shoes, put my few hairpins in tighter, so as not to lose them, and lay down, covering myself with the muslin from head to foot to keep off the mosquitoes.) I think that it must have been a party for married women only, as practically all the visitors brought babies with them. They all sat on mattresses on the roof, in a clump, and talked and talked.

At first their conversation seemed to be quite ordinary chatter of their kind. I lay still with my eyes closed, and tried to put their sentences together. As they all spoke at one and the same time, it was very difficult to catch anything in particular. Then I saw someone coming over to me. It was Keremah. She stood and looked at me, and pulled the muslin back to make sure I was asleep. When she replaced it she left a good opening for the mosquitoes to get at me!

Keremah went back to the others, and they all drew closer together. Their conversation grew decidedly more interesting, and I strained my ears to hear what I could of it. Their gesticulations were dramatic and made it easy to follow what they were saying. It was evidently about the Qeshlah and the happenings of the fateful 13th. One woman, whose voice I could distinguish, had all the news, and gave a glowing account of the deaths of the *Sahibs*. . . . Then there was a lot about some man who was evidently a ringleader in the trouble. He had been a levy, who had been imprisoned for some misdemeanour, but had been released before his time by some other A.P.O.—not Wrigley—and had joined the tribesmen. But for him, it seemed, the attackers of the Qeshlah might have contented themselves with merely looting.

I also heard for the first time that there was fighting in the neighbourhood of Baqubah Camp; but it was impossible to make out with what result.

Coffee and cigarettes were then handed round to the guests. I nearly decided to wake up and join them on the advent of coffee, but stifled my desire and remained still. Some of the women began to go, but others stopped on much longer. Then, somewhere about midnight, the noise of firing was heard. I had not been asleep yet, and at the firing I no longer pretended to be sleeping. I sat up and asked what the shooting was for.

Only the sentries, was the answer. But I noticed that the remaining guests hurriedly departed the way they had come, across the garden-wall to their various homes. Sheikh Majid could be heard going to his secret room with a lamp and unlocking the door. When he came out, his wife called down to him. The reply was evidently satisfactory, for the women now all settled themselves for the night and paid no more attention to the firing.

What we had first heard seemed to be at some little distance; but it was not so much the sound of that which disturbed me as the noise of people running in the streets, and the discharge of occasional rifles as they went. It may be that they were still testing new weapons; or perhaps they were firing to give themselves courage—probably the latter.

Altogether it had been a night of trouble and disturbance, and I do not know how I managed to sleep after all. But there was this about it. I was yet in the early days of my captivity, and I still thought that it would only be two or three more days, five at the most, before the British came to rescue me. Had I known that it was to have lasted for nearly a month—a month of continual terror, hardship, and misery—before any help came, I am certain that I should never have been able to struggle against the fever and dysentery which were getting hold of me. Let the reader imagine a white woman alone in a strange place, among strange people with a strange tongue, at first not know-ing whether they were at heart friends or enemies, and then realising only too well that they were enemies. Then carry your imagination farther and see this woman, after being there a day or two, with noth-ing whatever to do but wait and hope, coming to realise or at least to believe that there was no hope. Such was my plight.

CAPTAIN WRIGLEY WITH A GROUP OF ARABS.

ARAB LEVIES.

CHAPTER 12

A Mystery-Man; and Something
From the Clouds

There was nothing particularly worthy of note in the early part of the following day, 16th August, and the hours in consequence seemed to crawl along with painful slowness; and the whole day passed with but one incident to stamp it on my memory. That incident, however, had a most unnerving and terrifying effect upon me. It will no doubt seem trivial in the telling; but to me at the time it was a terrible experience. I can offer no explanation of its meaning, and it is as much a mystery to me now as it was then.

I was sitting in my room, where Keremah had left me for a moment with her baby and some of the other women, when suddenly a strange man entered. There was no warning, such as had always been given previously when a man was coming. The women got up and went away directly. Keremah came back hurriedly and fetched the baby, glaring at me as though she could kill me. Then I was left alone with the man.

Who he was, I have no idea. He was tall, dark, and better dressed than the average man of Shahraban, having a brightly coloured silk *kafiyah* wound round his head. He had rings on his fingers and a silver-hilted dagger stuck in his belt.

At first I thought that he had come with some message for me. But this was evidently not so, for he made no *salaam* and did not utter a word. He simply leant against the wall opposite to me and stared, with his arms folded. He seemed to find something humorous about me, for there was a fixed smile upon his face all the time. Just at the beginning I was more puzzled than frightened. When he continued to stand and stare, however, I grew more and more nervous, and my heart started thumping violently. Still I tried my hardest to show no outward signs of fear.

The man produced a cigarette, lit it, and began to smoke, staring at me unceasingly. After about five minutes of this I felt that I could bear it no longer. I looked at everything in the room except him, and then studied the floor. By now I was quite losing control over myself. At every movement which the man made I gave a start. I have been asked since why I did not get up and run out of the room. Had I thought of that at first I would have done so; but afterwards my terror was too great to let me move.

I suppose in reality my ordeal only continued for about ten minutes in all, but it seemed very much longer. At last I saw a woman passing at the other side of the courtyard, and I called 'Jumeila, Jumeila!' The woman went on unheeding; but my cry had the desired effect. The man stood away from the wall, lit another cigarette, and swaggered slowly out.

The same thing happened three or four times afterwards, but none of the man's subsequent visits put such a strain and tension on every nerve as the first did. I realised that the only thing to do was to keep my dignity, and on no account to show any sign of fear. This I outwardly did (with the exception of the first time), sitting still as stone, and if my eyes happened to glance in his direction, showed no more interest than if he had been one of the innumerable flies crawling up the mud walls. However, it took me quite a long time to recover my calm after the first intrusion of this mysterious stranger. The whole of the next day, whenever the door creaked, I caught hold of the nearest woman, determined not to let her go if there was another man come to watch me. They only said '*Latraf*' (do not fear), but that was just what I could not do.

My fourth day of captivity, 17th August, was the last on which I have a distinct recollection of the order of events. I remember the incidents which followed, but I had lost count of the days. On this fourth day more women came by the score to have a look at me. Some of them brought their spindles with them and sat spinning; but the majority sat idle and smoked cigarettes while they stared. All, however, chattered busily the whole while.

In the evening Hamid came and gave me another great surprise. He told me that my cook and Armenian boy were alive in a house in the town, and would like to come and see me. I was astonished, after the graphic account which he had given me of their killing. I asked eagerly if anyone else were alive from the Qeshlah. No, he assured me, everyone else had been killed who was there.

Later on two very bedraggled and depressed-looking creatures came into the women's courtyard. They were dressed in long blue overalls, and it was not until they came near that I recognised them as cook and Gosdan. At first they seemed afraid to speak. Then they plucked up courage to tell me how they had been stripped of every stitch of clothing in the Qeshlah, and had effected their escape in this condition into a neighbouring garden, where they hid throughout the night. Early in the morning, when the cold drove them out, they made their way to a house, where they received the minimum of clothing and food.

I asked them how they were getting on for food now. Both said that they had had enough since they had been prisoners. But when I asked them what they got—in the faint hope that, if their fare was better than mine, they would save me some!—they only appeared to have the same as I had been getting. Their diet was Arab bread, rice, tomatoes, and dates, which was suitable enough for them. Unhappily it did not suit me; by now I was thoroughly upset with this food and the unboiled water.

I put my usual question to them, 'Have you heard whether we are going to be killed?'

Cook was not encouraging. 'Perhaps we are, *Memsahib*,' he said, 'I don't know.'

The Armenian boy was much more hopeful. If they were going to kill us, he argued, why should they not have done so today or yesterday or the day before? Why should they have kept us alive so long?

There was some sense in this, though what Gosdan said cheered me very little at the time. Thinking it over later, I came to the conclusion that what the Arabs were doing was waiting to see whether the British were coming or not. If they were not coming, then I was sure that Sheikh Majid was not going to keep me in his house for an indefinite time.

Cook and Gosdan did not stay long, but left, expressing the wish that they hoped to be allowed to come and see me again.

I think that it was on the morning following their visit that the next incident occurred. I had pulled my bed into the shade of the date-palms on the roof. (Sometimes the Arab boys would climb these trees, a stout belt fastened round their waists and the trunk of the tree, by which they would pull themselves up to the top, and select the ripest fruit to stow away in their clothing.) I always delayed going down into the courtyard as long as the sun permitted, so as to shorten the eternal monotony of the day down below; and, besides, it was so much quieter on the roof than in the courtyard. So I was still upstairs when I caught the sound of an aeroplane in the distance. There was no mistaking the hum of the engine. A tremendous hope surged in me, and looking all round the roof, I saw to my amazement that no one was watching me. This was very strange, as there was always somebody left to keep guard over me, though why I cannot think. Even if I had cherished such a desperate thought as to attempt to escape, how far was I likely to get? I knew it was impossible.

But now when I heard the hum of the engine, the thought did come into my mind. In some vague way rescue seemed at hand as soon as I saw the plane. I leapt up and snatched the muslin covering from my bed, waving it frantically. It was white, and I felt sure that it must be seen. I continued to wave it as hard as I could, straining every nerve in my body to prevent myself shouting; my one overwhelming impulse at that moment was to shout my very loudest.

I kept on waving until the plane was right out of sight. It had not seen me, for surely, if it had, it would have turned and circled round to show that my signals had been observed. When it had gone, I sat down on the roof, utterly depressed and miserable. I suppose the plane had been at too great a height to notice me, and my faint hope of rescue had deserted me. It was a bitter moment.

When I looked up, I discovered that I had been watched all the time. Angry faces were glaring at me over the wall. I had done for myself now, I felt sure. A woman came up and told me to go downstairs at once; and I could do nothing but obey, but I knew that I was being discussed freely, and in none too pleasant a fashion. I could hear the word 'Madam' very frequently, and then would come that annoying click of the tongue and teeth and passing of the palms of the hands over one another by which so often the Arabs express their disgust.

Even my pitcher of water, which was nearly always put near me, was not there that morning. Only those who have been desperately thirsty in a hot sun-scorched land know the longing for a drink of water when there is none by; and I was really afraid that I was not going to get any. I went to the women and asked humbly, in my best Arabic, for some water. Each of them suggested that another should get it for me, but no one went, until at last Jumeila, as usual, was the one to fetch it. Even she only brought the pitcher and put it down on the step, leaving me to take it to my room. Evidently she was also too annoyed with me to come near.

The time went by terribly slowly. I felt like a culprit in disgrace, avoided by everyone. Not even Hamid paid me a visit. It was not until the afternoon that Jassim came in. He brought with him some dates, which he gave to me—the first thing I had to eat that day. It is true that I was beginning to get used to eating very little, and the less I ate the less I seemed to want. Occasionally a feeling of hunger came over me; but it soon passed off. Perhaps it was the fact of smoking much more than I had been used to dulled my desire for food. I had got into the Arab women's habit of smoking a lot during the day; and there were the cigarettes which Sheikh Hassan gave me to fall back upon.

The coming of the aeroplane, though it brought me into trouble, had an amusing sequel later in the day. An old man, one of the relatives of Sheikh Majid, who lived opposite—a kind of albino, with white hair, very pasty skin, and little blue, red-rimmed eyes—came through into the women's quarters in a violent hurry, holding in his hand a small round white ball. With him were a number of other men, armed to the teeth and bristling with rifles, knives, and daggers. With him, too, was Hamid, who came up to me and said: '*This* has been found near the Qeshlah. An aeroplane passed over this morning and dropped it.'

This, was a tennis-ball!

I explained that it was nothing but one of the balls with which we played on the court, and I took it from them and bounced it on the floor. Immediately every one sprang back terrified, evidently thinking that it was going to explode.

In spite of my feeling of being in disgrace I had to laugh. The thought of the careful way in which they had brought the ball into the house, probably afraid all the time that it might burst and kill them on the way, was too ludicrous. It is very strange how these Arabs' minds, which in some ways are so clever and cunning, in others are so small and foolish.

When they saw me laughing they were satisfied, and all laughed too, except the old albino man, who went on muttering and scowling at me.

It must have been on the night of this same day that a man called Iskender first came to see me. I do not remember having actually seen him before except in the Qeshlah on the 13th. I knew, however, that he had been in Wrigley's office and was an interpreter—though

91

Wrigley had no need of an interpreter, speaking Arabic quite well himself.

Iskender was an Egyptian, tall and rather stout, with good teeth, black curly hair, and a little moustache. When I had seen him previously he had been dressed in a buff-coloured silk coat, of European cut, and a red *fez*. Now he was in Arab clothes. My first feeling was one of doubt whether he had come as a friend or a foe. However, he sat down and told me how he too had escaped from the Qeshlah. It appeared that he had narrowly escaped being killed, as one of the tribesmen had galloped towards him preparing to shoot. But a friend of his among the townspeople had saved his life by giving the tribesman money, and so he had been spared.

We spoke in English, and did not have much conversation; Hamid was standing near, and, even if I had felt certain of Iskender's sympathies, I dared not speak too openly. I could not resist, however, asking the inevitable question, 'Do you think I am going to be killed?'

Iskender could not say. It all depended.

Did he think the British were coming? He did. But when? 'I do not know. Perhaps in a week or ten days.'

He added: 'You signalled to an aeroplane this morning. Why did you do it? It was very unwise.'

We talked a little more; then Iskender took his departure with Hamid. I afterwards found that I had no reason whatever to doubt his loyalty. He was an Egyptian Christian, and had no sympathy with Mohammedan Arabs. As will be seen later, he behaved with extreme kindness to me.

This night, as I lay awake on the roof, I heard noises which puzzled me. They were not the sound of rifle-shots, for these were only too familiar to me, but seemed like the distant boom of guns. The sound was repeated several times during the night, and each time I felt more certain that it was guns, and that it came from the Baghdad direction. Could it be the beginning of our rescue? I fell asleep at last with these thoughts in my mind.

CHAPTER 13

A Night in the Date-Season

It must have been the next morning Sheikh Hassan entered the women's quarters and announced to me, 'The Sergeant of the Grass Farm is coming to see you.'

The women promptly drew their *abbas* over their faces and withdrew. When all had left, the sheikh and Hamid brought Baines into my room, supporting him on either side, for he could still only just stagger and looked terribly ill. His arms were bound up in the same dirty rags as before, and he had on the same bloodstained shirt. He sat down on a seat, and now for the first time we were able to take stock of one another. I had only just seen him for the first time in the Qeshlah, and the second time, when I visited him in the men's quarters, I had hardly much opportunity of really taking in details.

John Baines—who is still, happily, alive—is a man of about twenty-four years of age, of medium height, clean-shaven, with fairish hair and blue eyes. He looked, as I have said, terribly ill, and it seemed a miracle to me that he should be surviving even then, with that awful-looking 'doctor 'to attend him, and those unclean rags to bind up his wounded arms. Yet, weak as he must have been with the blood he had lost, and considering the terrible experiences he had been through, he was wonderfully brave and calm.

Sheikh Hassan left us, but as he went he said to Hamid, 'Don't leave the prisoners.' So it seemed evident that we were not to be allowed to discuss anything privately.

I asked him to tell me what had happened to him at the Qeshlah and after. This was his tale.

When the insurgents rushed the Qeshlah, he was standing by the outer wall, among the shrubs, reloading his rifle. Two of the tribesmen sprang over the wall, almost on the top of him, and pulled at his rifle. He clung to it, but one slashed at his arm with a knife, laying it open, while the other struck his hand and made a terrible wound. Then he received a stab in the stomach and lost consciousness. What brought him to, he said, was the sound of my screaming. I knew that I screamed my hardest and loudest, but I never imagined that it had been so piercing as to be heard above all that awful din! Then a *bedou* (tribesman) came and stood over his body. He never moved, and the *bedou* took him for dead, but gave him a sword-thrust in the shoulder nevertheless, to make sure I suppose.

Poor Baines said he remembered seeing the sword descending and feeling the thrust, and that his thought was, 'Thank God, this is the end!' He lost consciousness a second time, and when next he was aware of what was going on around him, the Qeshlah was in flames, the neighbouring bushes had caught fire, and his own clothes were smouldering. He tried to move, but fell back exhausted. Then he heard two solitary shots, and said to himself: 'That must be Captain Buchanan! He has shot his wife and himself!'

The next thing that he remembered was that he was pulled out from among the shrubs by some of the townspeople and taken along the road to the town—the same road which passed the garden where I had hidden—and so by the narrow path past the coffee-shop to Sheikh Majid's house. Here he was laid down on a mattress. He asked for some water, which was given to him; and then he was left for the night. The next morning his wounds were dressed. That is to say, they were smeared over with that same 'Mobile oil' which had inspired me with such disgust, and bound up with rags. And there in a corner room in the men's courtyard he had lain until now.

I could not help exclaiming, 'Oh, poor Mr. Baines! It is Mr. Baines?' I added.

'Yes, they all call me "Sergeant," but I never was a sergeant in the war, and am not now. My name is just John Baines.'

'Well, Mr. Baines. Have you got a comb? I can't get my hair out of tangle.'

Yes, he had a comb, which Hamid had found for him. He would send it over to me. After that we shared the precious comb. At least, it remained with me, he sending for it from time to time.

All this time Hamid had remained with us, listening to what we said, and drinking in every word. Now he moved to the door of the courtyard, and this gave the opportunity for a few more private words.

'Do you think that we are going to be killed?' I asked hurriedly.

'I am sure I could not tell you,' Baines replied.

'I am certain we are'—not a very cheering thing to say to a man half-dead, I fear. 'What are you going to do if they begin?'

'Oh, I don't know. I shall try to put up a show; but I can't use either arm at present. They are pretty painful, especially at night when I can't sleep.'

'I do wish I could do something for you.' Then, putting into words the one hope that filled both our minds: 'Do you think the British will ever come?'

'I should think they are bound to, when they hear about the Qeshlah.'

'But when?'

'I couldn't say. Perhaps in a few days.'

'Do you know, I am sure I heard guns last night.' I went on to tell him of the curious sounds I had heard the night before. I was positive that it was the booming of guns, and from the direction of Baghdad. But he was equally positive that he had heard nothing of the kind; and the pain in his arms had kept him awake nearly all night. Our rescue was not so near at hand as that, he thought.

'But what I am frightened of,' I continued, 'is this. Even if they don't kill us now, when the British come they will, so that we shall not be able to tell what has happened.'

'Yes, I never thought of that,' he admitted.

Now, however, Hamid came back to us, and we were compelled to talk of unimportant things. Soon afterwards Baines went back to his quarters. Before he left I asked him to come and see me again, which he promised he would do next day, if he were allowed.

I do not recollect anything else of particular interest that happened this day. The heat was terrific, as it was throughout the whole time of my imprisonment. I would have called it unbearable, except that I had perforce to bear it. It was now the time of the date-season, and was no doubt very good for the dates. During this glaring, awful heat, which lasts usually about two weeks, the dates ripen.

The greatest trial of all in this fierce heat was the lack of really cool drinks. Those who have been in Mesopotamia, or in similar climates, will appreciate what this means. There was, of course, water; but the only time that this was cold was early in the morning, when my pitcher had stood on the wall of the roof all night to catch the breeze. Then it was icy-cold and—canal-water though it was—delicious. The construction of these *hibbs*, or pitchers, enables them to be cooled when there is some agency like the night-breeze to assist in the process. They are of porous earthenware, allowing the water to percolate through.

My evening meal of bread and tomatoes was not brought me this day, so when I went to the roof I lay down and tried to sleep. The women had all brought their mattresses on the roof earlier than usual, and sat together in a clump, talking together in very low tones, of which not a word that I caught could I understand. At length they ceased talking, and began to settle themselves for the night.

We were not destined, however, to get rest so soon. I had noticed that there had been extra noise that evening in the men's quarters, and that in our part of the house a huge wooden pole had been pushed up against the little garden-gate to barricade it. Now, all of a sudden, came the sound of shots in the distance, and almost immediately there was a rush and a buzz in the men's quarters. The women all sprang up in great haste from their mattresses and ran to the wall which overlooked the other courtyard, uttering a sort of war-cry, a high shrill scream, punctuated by patting the palm of the hand rapidly against the mouth all the time. Its effect is very weird. They kept this up until all the men who were in the courtyard were fully armed, and had gone out into the road in single file.

I kept on asking the women what it was that was happening; but I could get no satisfactory reply out of them in their excited state. Then at last Hamid came along, and I questioned him. He said it was the tribesmen trying to get into Shahraban to loot the townspeople. 'Will they come to this house?' I asked.

'No,' he said; 'they will loot the Jews' houses principally, but they will not come to us because Sheikh Majid is a cousin of Sheikh Hamid, the head of the tribesmen. Don't fear, sister,' he concluded. 'We have more than a thousand rifles and plenty of ammunition and strong men to fight. And if they are killed the boys will go out. All boys here learn to shoot early.'

I did not exactly see the necessity of this last reinforcement, for if they were the same tribesmen who had attacked the Qeshlah they were not over eight hundred strong.

After a while the women grew calmer and lay down in a line along the wall and the edge of the roof. I went back to my bed and lay down also, watching the wonderful sky, hoping for sleep. But there was more excitement to come. A volley of shots rang out quite close in the garden beside our house. Terrified, I sprang from my bed and ran in among the women. I threw myself down flat beside someone on her mattress, and pulled at her quilt till I had covered my head. The odour that arose from that bevy of women was truly appalling, but I felt that I must have company. I was too frightened to speak, and lay quite still. It seemed to me that more fighting and shooting was beyond my endurance. The women kept calling to one another in hushed voices, all talking, yet all continually saying, '*Sh! Sh!*'

Sheikhs Majid and Hassan and the rest of the men must have been out still, and there was no sound of anyone about in the men's quarters. Baines must have been left all alone, but I am afraid that I did not give a thought to him at the moment!

The firing seemed now to be right under the garden wall, and an occasional shot went whistling over the roof. (There is a certain fascination in the whistle of a bullet overhead, I have since thought, but I certainly did not appreciate it just then.) The women were all lying flat and still, talking, but more quietly than before. I crept closer to the one beside whom I had thrown myself, and pulled more of her quilt over me, regardless of the unpleasant odour. I kept calling to myself, 'Billy,' and praying that he might come and not leave me again; and somehow I seemed actually to believe that he would come.

I never had such a feeling of comradeship for these Arab women as on this night, when the shooting was so close to us, and they were obviously so frightened too. I wanted to be one of them, even felt that I was one. It was not now, 'Am I going to be killed?' but 'Are we going to be killed?' and that made all the difference. But gradually, as the firing died down and went farther away, my repulsion returned. I became more acutely conscious of the horrible smell, and thought of bad eyes and sores which I was quite likely to contract from my bedfellow. I believe it must have been Barkah next whom I lay. I certainly had not stopped to choose when I threw myself down, but just got as quickly as I could into the nearest space available. Now as soon as it was comparatively quiet, I got up and returned to my camp-bed, where at least there was pure air around me.

The men did not return to the house that night, but we had no repetition of the excitement. On the following day I learnt that the firing had been the townspeople shooting at the *Bedouin*, who had broken into their gardens and were stealing their dates from the trees. It seemed a tremendous fuss about a few dates! But I did not then realise the value of a date-palm and what the fruit means to the Arab.

CHAPTER 14

Sheikh Hamid of the Beni Tamim

On the morning following the tribesmen's attempt on the date-crop there was a hurried tidying-up of the women's quarters, which clearly showed that something unusual was about to happen. My room was swept—an event indeed!—the mattresses were put neatly in a corner, and chairs were set in a row. I asked Jumeila what it was for, and she told me that Sheikh Hamid was coming to see me.

I heard the news with very mixed feelings. Why should this tribes-man chief want to see me? Could I expect any alleviation of my lot from his visit, or would it make matters still worse? As soon as I heard the door in the courtyard creak, I went and stood in the corner of my room farthest away from it.

Sheikh Hamid entered, accompanied by a number of lesser *sheikhs* and by his cousin, Sheikh Majid. The latter told me not to be afraid. Sheikh Hamid, he said, was the biggest man of the tribesmen, and had more power than anyone else. (I grew accustomed to this—every new *sheikh* was the biggest man of all!) They waited until I had sat down on my bed, and then seated themselves on the chairs facing me.

Sheikh Hamid was a man of medium height, with a very sallow face, in which the most notable feature was the eyes. They were vivid brown, and the whites showed up very prominently, giving him a cu-rious hunted look. But, all the same, he had a manner which I liked, and of all the sheikhs with whom I came into contact he was the one in whose presence I felt safest.

This Hamid, I afterwards learnt, was a chieftain of the Beni Tamim, that great tribe of Arabs who came from the Arabian Peninsula some time before the Mohammedan period, and in the days of the prophet seemed to have been in virtual possession of Mesopotamia. The Beni Tamim are still scattered all over Mesopotamia, one of their strong-

98

Arab types.

Arab religious procession.

holds, according to Miss Lowthian Bell (*The Arab of Mesopotamia*), being the plains below the Persian hills—which includes, I suppose, the Shahraban neighbourhood. Owing to Persian influence, they belong to the Shiah sect of Mohammedans, unlike their former masters, the Turks.

I am afraid that I made a foolish start in my interview with Sheikh Hamid.

'Why did you let your men kill my *Sahib*?' I blurted out.

A long explanation followed, which went through the boy Hamid, who was present as interpreter. The sheikh protested that he was bitterly sorry for what had happened. Had he been there at the time, it would never have occurred. The Qeshlah. indeed, might still have been looted, but none of the *Sahibs* would have been killed. (I wonder if Sheikh Hamid thought the *Sahibs* would have stood by and watched the Qeshlah being looted?) He had been away in Persia when the attack was made, and came back post-haste as soon as he heard of it; but it was then too late.

He wept a little as he made his protestations. How easy it seems for the Orient to summon up tears! I believe, nevertheless, that he was genuinely sorry.

He then asked me if I wanted for anything. Yes, I said eagerly, I must have some clothes. I had nothing to wear except what I had on. Then, too, I did not get enough to eat. Could I have some milk to drink, and could I go in safety to my billet to fetch some of my things away?

Sheikh Hamid appeared surprised at my requests and had a conversation with his cousin, who had evidently told him that I had all that I wanted. Sheikh Majid turned to me and said, 'But I told you to ask for what you wanted!'

'Yes, and I have asked daily,' I answered, 'but what I ask for is never given to me.'

Sheikh Hamid told his cousin that I must have clothes and more food. The other protested much and, I have no doubt, gave him to understand that I was lying. But the chieftain promised that more food should be furnished for me, and that I should be allowed to visit my billet.

The conversation went back to the happenings of 13th August. 'Oh, Sheikh Hamid,' I exclaimed, 'why weren't you there that night, if you could have saved their lives? Why did you let them be killed like that? '

I went rambling on, reproaching him with the death of my *Sahib*, who was not in Shahraban as a fighting man. He had done his fighting in the Great War, and had only been here to help the Arabs with their water. He was their friend, not their enemy.

I was crying now, and so too were nearly all the men. When I saw this, I made an effort to control myself.

The interview continued for some considerable time, but I cannot remember anything more that was said. Sheikh Hamid repeated his promise, that I should have more food and be allowed to get some clean clothes. I thanked him. Then, as he was preparing to leave, he put out his hand. But had my life at that moment depended on it, I could not have brought myself to shake hands with one in whose veins ran the same blood as that horde which had brought all this sorrow upon me. So passing my hand over my eyes, I pretended not to have seen it.

So he departed, with his attendant *sheikhs*. Sheikh Majid stayed behind and called Jumeila to him. After he had spoken to her she went away, and soon afterwards returned, bringing a dish of watermelon to me. I took some of this and ate it, but not as much as I should have liked, for I knew that they were supposed to contain cholera germs.

So it really looked as if a fresh start had been made after Sheikh Hamid's visit. Cook and Gosdan came to me and said that they had been told, if I wanted them, they would be permitted to stay in the house and look after me. I impressed on cook that the one essential for me was to have my drinking water boiled, and, as I was going to be allowed milk, he must see that was boiled also.

Alas! my hopes in this respect were vain. I only had two bowls of milk, and they were both unboiled. Nor was the water boiled. Cook continually said that he could find no wood, and no one would give him enough to make a fire. The natives use very little wood, it being very scarce, but keep their fires going principally with the dried droppings of the cattle from the roads. I had to continue on unboiled water; and by this time I had dysentery very badly.

The boy Hamid came to me, too, and repeated that cook was to be allowed to stay in the house and prepare food for me. I protested that it was absurd to talk of preparing food, when he knew that there was no food to prepare. 'I don't know, sister,' he replied. 'That is what Sheikh Majid says.' Then he said that it had been arranged to give the prisoners one *rupee* four *annas* each day, out of which to buy their own food and cigarettes.

Perhaps a daily one *rupee* four *annas* does not sound so inadequate. But in the hands of Hamid, who did the shopping, it did not appear to go much farther than four *annas* should. He actually brought the money and showed it to me the first day. This was the one and only time that I saw my pittance, and, so far as I could make out, it only arrived, as a rule, every other day. It was expended this day on a scrap of sugar, a Little tea, and a tiny chop. The chop was made into a stew by cook. When I asked Hamid in the evening to tell cook to prepare a meal, he answered, 'No more money left, sister, all gone! '

I had received none of my usual dates or tomatoes that day, nor anything beyond the piece of watermelon, so that really I was no better off for food than I had been before. And the pittance never went any farther than it did that day. I told Hamid to buy a tin of cigarettes for me in the *bazaar* with the next day's money. I knew that a tin of Virginians could be got there for one rupee four *annas*, and they would be better for my throat than the Arab cigarettes.

As for clean clothes, the landlord of our billet had evidently been told to bring me some, for a small bundle of things arrived, tied up in a saddle-cloth. I opened it with anxiety and found in it—one shoe, a collection of dirty rags, which had been used by cook for his pots and pans in the kitchen, and one object which I did not recognise at once. It looked like another dirty rag. I shook it out and discovered it to be a former frock of mine. It had obviously been tried on by Arab women, and it was both torn and soiled. I hardly cared to use it, even if it was washed, and was on the point of throwing it away, as I thought I should be able to pick out several other frocks when I went to the billet. It was lucky that I kept it!

The next day Sheikh Hassan came in and told me that I was going to be taken to the billet. I felt very pleased. Now at last, I thought, I should get something clean into which I could change!

CHAPTER 15

I Revisit our Billet

When I was ready—and it did not take me long to prepare for this first excursion of mine since I had been brought to my *harem-prison*—I went through the men's quarters, and found waiting for me at the gate Sheikh Hassan, the boy Hamid, Fahal, and several other men. All were armed, with the exception of Hamid and Fahal. We went out into the narrow lane which led from the house, and at once I had a foretaste of the ordeal through which I must go. A number of men began to collect round us, all carrying arms. Feeling exceedingly frightened, and unable to face more shooting, I begged to be allowed to go back again. But my escort would not hear of it. Evidently women out there are not privileged to change their minds as we are! So I was obliged to go on. As we neared the familiar coffee-shop, I saw a large crowd. When they observed me, they came up close and gathered round, talking and shouting at the top of their voices.

Desperately I clutched at the *abba* of one of our party, and pulled it until it came off, and wrapping it round, so as to cover my head, felt a certain amount of protection in that. The crowd, however, kept pressing round, and as we reached the front door of the billet it became worse. The door was locked, and we tried it in vain, so there was nothing to do but wait until the landlord should arrive with the key. I felt frantic, and catching hold of Sheikh Hassan, cried: 'Send them away, oh, *do* send them away, they will kill me!' He and some of the other men ordered the crowd to keep back, without any other effect, however, than to make them surge more closely round us. Then someone fired a shot into the air. I screamed loudly and tried to hide myself beneath Hassan's *abba*. He pushed me back against the door and stood in front of me, shouting to the mob to keep away.

I do not know how long it was before the landlord arrived, but it seemed ages. At last he was there, with the key in his hand, and unlocked the door. Running in, I got behind it until our party had entered and it was locked again from inside. I cannot describe what a relief it was to have the door between me and that awful horde of yelling Arabs. Yet it was a dreadful feeling, too, to be shut up alone with this party of strange men, and I would have given anything to be back at Sheikh Majid's, in the women's quarters. Nothing would have induced me to come had I known it was going to be like this. I had somehow imagined it would have been simply a case of a walk here and a walk back, just getting the things I wanted from the house.

Still, here I was, back in the billet which I had never expected to see again. Going into the courtyard, I looked round. . . . My eyes suddenly blinded with tears. Could this be the same place which I had left on the morning of the 13th? The little square of garden, about which we had such hopes, was flattened out, with not a sign of green in it. The yard was littered with boxes, bits of wood, old kerosene cans, broken china, straw, and paper.

I went into Billy's office. The lock had been broken off every drawer and cupboard, and all were lying open. Papers were strewn all over the floor, and the books had been torn across. I bent down and picked up some of the papers, glancing through them aimlessly, and began to put them together neatly. . . . My brain seemed numb. . . . Then I realised how useless a thing I was doing. There was no need for his office to be kept cool or tidy now!

I passed on into my *surdab*, from the door of which the lock had been torn, Like all the others. Not a single piece of furniture was left, it was entirely bare. The next *surdab* was just like it. Every room downstairs was in the same condition.

I went out again and looked down the well, it was dry. Boxes had been thrown down it, and on the top of one lay a dead chicken. Even the rope and bucket had been taken away.

I climbed upstairs and went first to the bedroom. It was unrecognisable. For a time I was dazed and quite forgot what I had come for, and sitting down on the bare floor I called faintly for Billy. The sight of my hopeless misery must have touched Sheikh Hassan's heart, for I could tell by his face he was extremely sorry that he had brought me here, knowing as he did in what a condition the billet would be. He bent over me and tried to lead me downstairs again. But I refused. There were the other rooms to see, and I went next into my little dressing-room. Here at least there was one piece of furniture still, the dressing-table. The looking-glass had been unscrewed and taken away, but the table was left. Pulling open a drawer, among the spilt powder I made a great find—about a dozen hairpins.

I suppose that to a male reader this seems a very trivial thing to rejoice over, in the midst of my agony, but a woman will understand how eagerly I picked them up and put them in my hair. By this time only three of my five were left, and each morning I had counted them, hunting all over the place if I had lost one. It used to cause great excitement among the women, who would join in the hunt. I wonder if they thought me mean? They had little idea what the pins meant to me. But they themselves were in the habit of hoarding up little bits of stuff of all kinds for which I could imagine no possible use; so perhaps they thought this was my particular little eccentricity.

I looked through the other drawers, hoping to find a pot of cream, which would ease the parched state of my skin, but there was none left. Glancing up, as I was going out of the room, I saw a panama hat hanging on a peg. Evidently it had been overlooked, and was doubly welcome as I had been without any head-covering all the time so far, and was in constant fear of getting sunstroke. Taking the hat down from the peg I put it on.

Next I went into the dining-room. It too had been stripped, except for the table, which had been thrown over on its side in a corner of the room, so probably they had made an attempt to carry it off, but had been unable to get it through the door.

I could not stay in this scene of desolation. Having never seen our billet empty before, the sight appalled me. The loss of material things is but a minor detail in comparison with that of those whom we can never replace. Yet, in a way, the sight of this bare place drove home my greater loss. I went downstairs, and turned my face to the wall and wept, feeling that nothing in the whole world mattered now. The landlord turned his face to the wall and wept also! And all the time, though I did not know it then, he himself had taken a great part of my stuff and removed it to his own house!

I asked him why they had done this thing. My *Sahib* had always been so kind to the Arabs; and what had I done that they should kill him and bring me back to this?

I do not believe that the landlord understood a word I said, but he wept all the more. Then he took me over to my store-room, and undid a padlock on the door. It was not my padlock, however, for I saw mine lying broken on the ground. We went in, and found just what I expected after seeing the other rooms. Only a few oddments were left. I can remember a number of lamp-chimneys on a shelf, some whole and others broken; a lot of smashed crockery on the floor; two oil-stoves; a few empty trunks, with their locks wrenched off; a suitcase and a cushion. I picked up the cushion, and asked to go.

The landlord assured me that he would not have had this happen in his house for anything, and cried again while he was waiting for Hamid to interpret to me.

It is extraordinary to think that this man who had taken such a big share of the loot himself could now pretend sympathy like this. How easily he could have put back at least a few clothes for me to find, and how much they would have meant to me! Not that I consider him any worse than Sheikh Majid, who, I was already convinced, had a lot of my things in that locked room of his. But of course I could not prove it, for I had not actually seen any of them taken in.

I went up to Sheikh Hassan and asked him to take me back, if I was to go back, but first to make every one go away outside. 'If that crowd comes round me again,' I cried, 'I shall die.'

I do not think that Hassan was much impressed by the possibility of my dying, but to me it seemed likely enough. I often wonder now why I did not die of sheer fright. I do not suppose that I have succeeded in impressing my readers sufficiently under what a terrible tension I was living. Let anyone try to picture it who has awakened in the middle of the night, in this safe country of England, and heard a strange noise. The heart beats fast, a drumming comes in the ears, and every nerve is strained to listen. Then it is realised that it was only a door creaking, or some other trivial thing. But I was living at a much higher pitch than this every moment of the day and night. What we dread most, I suppose, when we are alone, is another strange human being. I was utterly alone, always with the fear of these half-savage strangers, who were so close to me, always waiting for a sword-thrust, or to find myself looking down the muzzle-end of a rifle, and waiting, waiting, apparently without end.

Sheikh Hassan went out first through the street-door, and shouted to the mob to go away and stand at a distance, as I was frightened to come out while they were there. They withdrew a short distance, and Hassan told me to come out. The others of the party followed me. As soon as I was outside the mob began to press round us again, but I did not find it so bad now as before. Perhaps I was too utterly miserable to be frightened. Catching hold of Hassan's *abba*, I kept talking to myself, always to the same effect, praying that Billy would come back and stay by me. It seemed to give me strength to go on.

When we turned the corner, however, and were in the lane near Sheikh Majid's house, I suddenly felt so giddy that I could not proceed. I stopped and really thought I could not move another step. The men waited a while for me as I leant against the wall. Soon one of them took my arm to help me along. I pushed him away—I fear I must have given them a very poor idea of English manners—and forced myself to walk back to the house without assistance.

A horrible sensation of depression fell on me as I saw our quarters again. They looked dirtier and more wretched than ever, and I thought of all the monotony and weariness to which I was coming back. But the women bustled round me and put my bed on the roof, telling me to lie down, and Jumeila even came and sat near me, and fanned me as I lay. The women expressed their sorrow that my *Sahib* had been killed and my billet looted—though I expect that practically every one among them had some of my things! I was given some grapes, very big ones, from one and a half to two inches long, and as I ate them the women watched me curiously.

That night there was a wonderful new moon. It rose slowly, gleaming through the trees, and had just reached the top of the date-palms when I fell asleep for the first time. I did this early. So much crying and the strain of that afternoon had tired me out.

I woke up again, however, before very long. There was firing going on somewhere near, and people were moving about in the house. I asked if Hamid was still here, and they sent for him. When he arrived I asked whether the Bedouin were trying to break into the town. They could not possibly do so, he said. There were plenty of sentries, and walls had been built up at all the entrances of the town. It did not sound particularly comforting to me to hear this. If they had thought it necessary to barricade the town, they were obviously afraid of visits from the Bedouin, in spite of the strong men and the thousand rifles of which Hamid had boasted on the night of the last raid. However, there was nothing to do but go to bed again and try to sleep.

I dozed off, and awoke much later, to find the moon nearly overhead. I lay looking at the sky, which is always enchanting in Mesopotamia at this time of the year, with its marvellous star-display. There was no rifle-firing to be heard now; but I fancied that I could catch, in the far distance, that curious noise like the boom of guns which I had heard before. It was repeated several times at intervals, and I grew

107

more and more positive that it was guns. I wondered if Baines, who had not noticed it the other night, was awake now and could hear it. He would be sure to know, with his experience of the war. In my own mind I had scarcely any doubt. And so, thinking of the possibilities of a speedy rescue (or would it only mean a speedy death?), I went off to sleep again for the remainder of the night.

CHAPTER 16

The Phantom Guns

A pleasant surprise awoke me the next morning. There was a sound of barking, and suddenly my dog Scut sprang up beside me, and began licking my face. He seemed half-mad with joy at seeing me again; and I, for my part, was delighted to see him. He was looking very dirty, but nice and fat, so had evidently managed to get food somewhere. He jumped off the bed and made frantic dashes round the roof, then sprang up again, and so on, for a long time.

Anyway, his return was a great comfort to me, and I felt at least there was one friendly thing to whom I could talk. He kept up his gambols until I was ready to go down, and then followed me to the courtyard. His first occupation there was to chase the chickens, until I caught hold of him and made him lie down.

The Arab women could not understand my making such a fuss about a dog. When I poured out some water for him in my bowl, they said to me: 'Why give a dog water? If he wants any, he will go and find some.' And Hamid told me to wash the bowl seven times before I used it again myself; it was unclean now that a dog had drunk out of it.

To me the way in which these people treated animals was incomprehensible. I have spoken of the abominable cruelty of the child Huzain to birds, and I had often previously seen boys sitting in the *bazaar* pulling the feathers out of live sparrows; it seemed quite a hobby of theirs. The horses and donkeys were shamefully used. The Western idea of the Arab's love for his steed is very mistaken. With the exception of good mares, all I saw were utterly neglected, and the stick was laid on hard where there was apparently no need for it at all.

One day, I remember, one of the horses that had been stolen from the Qeshlah was brought into the women's courtyard. I recognised it as a grey belonging to Captain Bradfield. He now looked ill-kept and thoroughly ill-used. The English saddle was still on his back, and the poor beast appeared dead-beat, as if he had been ridden hard and far. I went up to him, patted him, and talked to him of his master, who had been a real lover of horses, and was especially proud of this grey. I was not allowed to make much fuss of him, however, for one of the Arabs came over, struck the horse a hard blow, and pulled him away from me to the other side of the trough. I went back to my room, not daring to take further notice of the horse, as it evidently only annoyed the Arabs. Besides, it was of course foolish of me to let them know I recognised him.

How the sight of that horse and saddle brought back memories to me! I sat in my room feeling more dejected and hopeless than ever.

Scut was very faithful to me, coming to see me constantly, but always slinking about in the daytime until he caught sight of me. Then he made a mad rush for me. His visits were short, however, for as soon as he moved away from me he disappeared for the rest of the day. I always thought he must have been kicked outside and dared not venture back. But at night he took to coming over the roof from some neighbouring house, and would generally sleep by my bed, growling if he heard anyone in the garden or Sheikh Majid paying a nocturnal visit to his locked room, which could always be detected in spite of careful unlocking and locking of the door. Sometimes a stray pariah dog came over the wall. If Scut's advances were received in a friendly spirit, a game would follow. But should the newcomer respond with a snarl, Scut would keep close to me and growl until the stranger had departed.

The same day that Scut turned up, I had another visit from Mr. Baines, who was as usual accompanied by Hamid. We had a little conversation in the latter's presence at first. I asked Baines how he got along with the one *rupee* four *annas*, and he told me that he had not had it, in fact, he had not even seen it once, though this did not seem to worry him—he was too ill to think of food. I inquired of Hamid why it was not given to Mr. Baines when the Indians all got it. I got the inevitable answer; Hamid did not know.

I told Baines that the money at least procured me my morning and afternoon tea, for which I was most thankful, and asked him if he would not stay and have tea with me. Hamid said that he would go and inquire whether this would be allowed. While he was away I seized the opportunity of telling Baines of the noise I had heard again last night. I was sure it meant good news, I declared. The British

110

Fruit grown in the gardens at Shahraban.

Baling presses at Shahraban.

were coming. I could most distinctly hear the *boom! boom!* of guns at intervals.

Baines was not convinced. He had been awake all the night, and had only heard men running in the streets, occasional rifle-shots in the distance, and the sound of horses' hooves in the neighbouring court-yard. It was in vain that I protested the noise was not any of these.

'Well, anyway, I am sure that the British will be here in a few days now,' I assured him.

He warned me that I had better not mention the name '*British*,' as anyone listening would be sure to understand that. So we agreed to speak only of 'the B.'s' in future.

I begged him to tell me any news he had heard in the men's quar-ters, but he assured me he had heard nothing at all.

'But you speak Arabic,' I went on, 'and can make out what they are talking about. You *must* have overheard something as to what is likely to happen to us.'

'No, they never mention anything like that when they are near me. And, when they do talk, they get so excited, and shout so loud and at such a rate, that I can't understand what it is all about.'

I was anxious to tell him about my visit to the billet, and what a ghastly experience it had been; but, before I could do so, Hamid came back to say that permission had been given for the Sergeant to stop and have tea with me. Tea was soon brought, and we went on with our talk. In Hamid's presence, however, it was impossible to say much, and we kept to unimportant things.

We tried to arrive at what day and what date in the month it was, but had both lost count of the days by now. There was nothing even to guide us to the hour except the sun. I had indeed grown quite expert at this, and could tell the hour almost exactly by the shadow cast by the roof on the courtyard below. If only I had had pencil and paper I could have kept count of the days too; but, though I asked for them repeatedly, they were never given to me. I wonder if my jailers thought that I might try to get a note through to Baghdad, and how they imagined I could manage it!

When Baines had left, the women came back and sat near me. This evening my insistence on the noises which I had heard being guns had had the effect of making me confident myself that the British were coming soon. I felt in a more normal frame of mind than since the day of the tragedy, and was emboldened to talk as I had not ventured be-fore. As the women sat round me, smoking and spitting, I smiled very sweetly at Jumeila, and explained to her what a repulsively dirty race they seemed to me, with many other very candid remarks. Poor Jumeila must have thought that I was saying something complimentary, for, by her expression, she was very pleased, and seemed thoroughly to approve of my ideas.

As a matter of fact, I really did think that some at least of the women would have looked quite nice if only they had been clean. But I certainly had not gone out of my way to compliment them. I felt the necessity of talking, because of my conviction that rescue was not far off, and for the same reason I let myself speak the more freely.

I went to bed about seven o'clock that night, full of anticipations of release, and tried hard to get to sleep soon. If only I could sleep now, I thought, and not wake until five the next morning, rescue would be ten hours the nearer; and what a relief that would be in this long agony of suspense!

Luckily I succeeded in getting off to sleep quite soon; but later Scut woke me up by his growling. I looked and saw a huge strange dog standing on the wall of the roof. I raised my arm quickly, and pretended to throw something at him, whereon he disappeared at once. But now I could not sleep again so easily. As I lay awake, I heard the same sound which had excited me before. I listened very intently this time, and noticed that it had come no nearer. I sat up in bed and strained my ears to catch it again. It came once more, and now I began to doubt. It was not so very much like guns as I had thought. Yet once more it came—and suddenly it dawned upon me that it was, after all, nothing but the stamping of horses' hooves on the mud floor of a neighbouring courtyard!

The disappointment was most cruel. How could I have been so foolish as to take the sound for guns? Now all my hopes were shattered, those fond hopes of seeing the British in a day or two. I had clutched, as a drowning man does at a raft, at my theory of guns; and the raft was gone. A greater depression than ever fell upon me, and if I slept again that night, it must have been from sheer exhaustion of nerves.

CHAPTER 17

Suspense and Terror

After this great disappointment the monotony of my life seemed far worse. It was broken by the occasional visits of Baines, who came to see me when he could. There was always the same hurry and bustle of the women to get away on his approach. And I fear I must have continually wearied him with the same question of how soon we were going to be killed. But his reply was always in the same comforting strain, 'I don't see why they have kept us so long if they are going to kill us.'

Each time we met we thought that the other would have some little bit of news which would be an excuse for hope. I was unjustly disposed, I am afraid, to blame him for not bringing some hopeful tidings. I knew that before the rising he had many friends among the Arabs, and had been able to mix with them freely. Some of them would surely come and tell him things, I thought, whereas I could not expect to hear much, being almost a stranger among the people, and knowing so little of the language.

Poor Baines! His wounds were still in a terrible state and made little, if any, progress. But through it all he was wonderfully plucky, saying with a true British Tommy's *sangfroid*, 'Well, I expect I shall have to have this arm off in the end.'

We were both suffering badly from mosquito-bites, and he was decidedly worse off than I in this respect. He had to grin and bear it, as his hands were useless, and he had not even the piece of muslin which I had. To be without a mosquito-net in a country like Mesopotamia is a mild—perhaps hardly a mild—form of torture.

Sheikh Hamid came to see me again two or three days after his former visit. I was partly prepared for this by the same rapid tidying-up as before, which always betided a visitor of importance coming to the women's quarters. He arrived, accompanied by some other *sheikhs* of the Azzah tribe, which had captured Captain H. I. Lloyd, Assistant Political officer, and Mr. J. Strachan, Assistant Irrigation officer, at Deltawah. Sheikh Majid was also of the party.

The *sheikhs* brought with them Iskender, who, after all were seated, told me that a letter had been brought for me from Captain Lloyd.

Where was it, I asked, and what was it about? But Iskender said that I must wait, they would give it to me presently.

The Arabs were talking together, mostly about me, I think. One man struck me particularly among them, and it was in a way quite a shock every time that he looked up. His eyes were blue—the first Arab eyes I had seen which were not brown, with the exception of those of the old albino relative of Sheikh Majid, and his eyes were so bleary that they might have been any colour—and he had fine clear-cut features, which reminded me of pictures of Christ. He carried, however, a very long curved sword in a highly decorated silver sheath.

As the sheikhs went on talking together, I asked Iskender what they were saying. Nothing of importance, he replied; he would tell me later.

Then at last two letters were produced from Captain Lloyd, one being for Iskender, the other for me. Mine, after a little note of sympathy for the loss of my husband, ran something as follows:—

'I think that it would be better if you came here. You would be more comfortable at Deli Abbas with us.'

My spirits rose rapidly. Anywhere would be better than this house that I was in, I thought.

Iskender asked me to show him my letter. I asked for his first. He hesitated, but finally agreed, and we exchanged letters. His was quite different from mine, and ended by telling him to be cautious how he acted, and to obey implicitly any orders he might receive.

I poured out a string of questions to Iskender. When should I go? Should I start at once with them for Deli Abbas? Had they an extra horse for me? What should I do about a *topee*? Would it be safe on the way, or were we likely to be attacked?

Iskender only answered the last question. No, it was not likely that any attack would be made, for the *sheikhs* were of opposite factions, and if they took me under their joint protection none of their followers would attack; and, besides, I had nothing to be looted.

I told Iskender that I was anxious to go, that I could not stay in this house any longer. Should I get ready? But he said I must wait until the sheikhs had talked things over. He added that if I went I should be safe, as Captain Lloyd was very much loved by the Arabs. This was reassuring, and although I had never seen Captain Lloyd myself, I knew that he and his wife lived at Deltawah, where he was A. P.O., and reputed to be, as Iskender had said, very popular with the Arabs. I afterwards learnt that his wife had been sent for by the Political Staff just before the rising, and so was away in safety when her husband and Mr. Strachan were captured.

I was impatient of the delay while the *sheikhs* discussed the situation, and asked Iskender to thank them for me and say I wanted to go to Deli Abbas. He turned to them and interpreted.

'Why,' exclaimed Sheikh Majid, 'do you not like it here? Do not my women wait on you, and do you not have what you want—tea and everything?'

I told Iskender that Sheikh Majid knew I had nothing that I wanted, and that everything was stolen from my billet, so that I had nothing left. What was the use of his pretending he did not know? I begged him, however, to put this in such a way as not to offend Sheikh Majid.

Iskender interpreted as he thought fit. The sheikhs had another discussion for a short while, and then went out and left me.

When I was alone I called Jumeila and asked for the piece of glass which acted as a mirror and was greatly treasured by the whole household. It was only a tiny broken piece; but still it was a looking-glass, and was better than nothing. I washed my face, did my hair—a much easier task since I had found those extra hairpins!—and was all ready in case the *sheikhs* would be starting soon.

But now the boy Hamid and some of the women came to see me, and began impressing on me the great dangers of the journey to Deli Abbas. According to them, I was sure to be attacked and killed on the way, for there were fierce tribesmen about. Captain Lloyd was by no means in safety. There was a price on his head, and he was certain to be killed, and I too if I were with him. Then Deli Abbas was a horrid place, with no proper houses, only reed-huts, and full of mosquitoes. Nor were there any women like the nice ones here. (I had my own opinion on this last point.) So they went on, and when I asked them why they were so anxious for me to stay, they urged how much better it was in Shahraban, where there were so many women and I had no work to do. Hamid said that Sheikh Majid was the biggest man— another of those 'biggest men'!—and had more power than anyone

116

else, and if I stayed with him ten or even twenty years I should be quite safe.

I refused to be persuaded, and asked if the Sergeant (Mr. Baines) were coming too. Hamid 'did not know, sister,' so I told him to go and say I was going to Captain Lloyd at Deli Abbas, and would Baines come too, if he could stand the journey, and I would do anything I could for him on the way.

While Hamid went with this message, the women continued advising me how dangerous it would be for me to go. They said that, if it were safe, Captain Lloyd would come and fetch me himself. I was quite at a loss to understand their persistency, as it had been sufficiently obvious that while I was there they had not wanted me with them at all, except perhaps Jumeila, who I thought liked me in a way; but, now that there was a suggestion of my going, they all seemed really anxious that I should stay. It was very strange.

Hamid came back, announcing: 'Not going for a long time, sister, not till sunset. No need to get ready yet. Rest, sister, it is a long journey, about twenty miles.'

So I was not to go yet, and as it was still the morning there were six or seven hours to wait. My heart sank. How could I find the patience to wait? I had been so full of excitement at the thought of going where there were other English people, where I should be at least in safety and have better food. I could not help thinking of the food, for it was a matter of no small importance in my state of illness.

However, there was nothing else to do but wait, and the appearance of a meal—an egg, Arab bread, and some dates, I remember it was—at least helped to pass the time. There was a tin of cigarettes too, brought by Sheikh Hassan, and at tea-time Baines came to see me, and we talked matters over, as much as we could with our usual audience.

The men's courtyard had been very quiet and deserted all that morning. Presently we heard the sound of many people coming into it, all in a state of great excitement. I caught the word 'Madam,' 'Madam,' repeated many times, and got very alarmed. I jumped at every sound, and felt that I must get away and out of sight.

'Where shall I hide, Baines?' I cried. 'I know that they have quarrelled about me and have come back to kill me?'

'Oh no, they haven't,' he said, 'they always carry on like that. Don't be frightened. They'll go soon. If Captain Lloyd knows you are at this house, they dare not kill you.'

I was not at all convinced. I was positive my last hour had come. I felt distracted, and asked Baines what was wrong with me.

He said that I must have got a very bad form of shell-shock. This was his usual diagnosis of what was the matter with me; and I suppose that really my nerves were in some such state. I tried hard to compose myself, but the constant repetition of 'Madam' was awful. Why on earth should they keep shouting my name unless something was going to happen to me? Baines went on reassuring me, and he did make me feel calmer. He always acted like a tonic, with his unfailing courage and cheerfulness. But the time came for him to go, and I was left alone with the women.

My terror returned as the noise continued in the men's courtyard. I looked round desperately and caught sight of Jumeila. I clutched at her and begged her to sit close to me and not to leave me. She complied, and tried to calm me by putting one hand over my heart and the other at my back, and pressing hard. This was their way of inducing the heart to beat more slowly! I do not know that it was very efficacious. My heart continued thumping hard, and I remember wondering how it could go on so long and not stop completely.

Then came the last straw. The Little boy Huzain ran in and told the women something about 'Madam.' There was a groan all round. It must really be my death-sentence this time. 'Bring Hamid,' I cried faintly. 'I want to tell him some things.'

Hamid was not to be found, however. At any rate, he did not come. So I sat waiting for the end. Ten minutes more, five minutes more, I kept thinking to myself. I felt like nothing so much as a mouse in a trap. The noise continued in the men's courtyard, the argument growing very heated at times. Suddenly Jassim entered and said that the *sheikhs* were coming.

I sprang up, determined to make one last despairing dash for life. I ran up the steps into Sheikh Majid's little room, of which the door led off mine. I had noticed several times before a deep grating and a window high up in a corner of the wall, just large enough for a person to crouch in, hanging on to the bars. I made straight for this, gave a spring half-way up the wall underneath the grating, and clutched at the bricks in a frantic effort to get a footing and hoist myself up. The women had run after me, and just as I was nearly out of reach caught hold of me and dragged me down and back into the room. I struggled violently to get free from them, and at last they let go and pulled their *abbas* across their faces. I saw Jassim standing by and clutched at him, imploring him to save me, not to let me be killed.

Then the courtyard door creaked, and the women hurried away. I got behind Jassim, still gripping him hard, and uttering, I am sure, piercing screams. Footsteps approached, and I could see, from behind Jassim, all the *sheikhs* standing in the room, and Iskender with them.

The Arabs seemed horrified and not a little frightened when they saw me. Sheikh Hamid, in particular, looked scared. I cannot wonder at this now. I could not get my breath, and I know I must have been making horrible noises in my throat. None of them spoke for a while, and then Iskender said: 'What is it? Do not be afraid.'

'Oh, I can't help it,' I gasped. 'This is awful. I thought—'

But I do not remember what I said. What I had thought, after all that commotion in the other courtyard, was that they were going to rush in with bare swords and set upon me; and the way that the women had dragged me out had confirmed my fears.

I was very sorry that I had made such a scene, and I really feel ashamed while describing it. I must have given them an extremely bad impression of the courage of Englishwomen, and made them think what a difference there was between our women and our men. But it was true that I could not help it. I was ill, and the constant suspense and terror had shattered my nerves. It was the 'shell-shock' from which Baines told me I was suffering!

I sat down on my bed, while Hamid brought me some water, and did my best to pull myself together. The Arabs continued silent for a time, and then began to talk in low whispers. Finally, Iskender told me that I was not going to Deli Abbas.

I made no protest, as I should have done before. I felt now that I did not care whether I went or stayed. What was the use of making a fuss? Nothing mattered at the moment. I was no longer afraid, only terribly unnerved. I sat with my head in my hands, trying to get calm.

Then Iskender asked me to write a note to Captain Lloyd, and tell him I would rather stay where I was.

This did rouse me a little. I said that it would not be true. I would much rather go to Deli Abbas.

'But you can't say that when you are staying here.'

'Why am I staying here?'

'They have discussed it, and you are to stay.'

This was final. I knew that Iskender was only acting as the mouthpiece of the *sheikhs*, and could but tell me what they said. When paper and pencil were brought, I asked him what I was to write. That I was staying with Sheikh Majid, he replied, and that I was comfortable and well treated.

No, I couldn't say that. He knew it was not the case that I was comfortable and well treated.

'Well, it would be most unwise of you to say that you are not,' he answered, which was no doubt true. I took the pencil and wrote:—

Dear Captain Lloyd,—It has been decided that I stay here (I hoped that he would understand from this that it was not *my* decision) and I am well treated.

I bitterly regretted afterwards that I agreed to write this, because the report spread in England that I was safe at Deli Abbas with Captain Lloyd and was being very well treated. It was my own fault that the latter untruth was believed. But what was I to do?

When I had finished the letter. Sheikh Hamid spoke to me and asked whether there was anything that I wanted. I told Iskender to say that I very much wanted clothes. He objected again that it would not be wise to say this. But this time I insisted. I could not go on as I was. So Iskender told the sheikh that I needed some clean clothes.

A long explanation by Sheikh Majid to Sheikh Hamid followed, at the end of which I was informed that some material would be brought to me so that I could make myself a dress. I knew, however, how much the promise was worth, so thought no more about it.

The *sheikhs* now left, and the women returned. Jassim came in and brought me a few unripe citrons, which were very refreshing and most welcome. He now came almost daily with some little offering, a handful of almonds or some extra fine dates, for which I was thankful. Such small kindnesses really touched me.

This evening the women did not sit round me as they usually did. I was by no means sorry to be thus ignored. I was not feeling well-disposed to them for the way they had pulled me out of hiding, after their protestations of sympathy with me. But I suppose it cannot have pleased them that I had been so anxious to leave their house and go elsewhere.

I was all the better contented to be left alone, for I felt extremely ill. My head was aching and I was burning all over. I went to bed early and slept right through the night without waking, unconscious of anything that went on around me.

CHAPTER 18

Fever; and More Suggestions of a Move

The next morning Gosdan brought me my tea on the roof early. The women were all near my bed discussing something together with great animation, and when I asked Gosdan what it was about he questioned them, and they chattered to him excitedly for a time. Then he turned and answered me. 'Your *Sahib* come and talk with you last night.'

'My *Sahib!* Who saw him? Why wasn't I awakened?'

'They say you see him and talk with him a long time, *Memsahib.*'

Then I realised that I must have been talking to Billy in my sleep or in delirium. Ever since that day of the 13th, I knew that I had, in times of great stress, called to him to come back to me. Somehow, too, I always expected that he would come, and it was a bitter disappointment each time. I was unaware, however, that I had called to him, much less seemed to talk with him, the previous night.

'What did I say?' I asked Gosdan.

He questioned the women, who were in a great state of excitement; but they could give no further information than that I had talked a lot with my *Sahib*. They were very anxious to know what he had said to me, what he looked like, and was he the same as when he was here in Shahraban? When I told Gosdan that I could remember nothing, it had all been a dream, they were very disappointed. They really appeared to think that I had seen him, and afterwards would ask me if he were coming again. They seemed genuinely sorry when I said 'No.'

I can recollect little of the next day or two. My body was in a burning fever, and I could take in little of my surroundings. I have a memory of Sheikh Majid standing over me and pressing my head very hard with his forefinger and thumb across the temples, praying all the time and, I suppose, invoking *Allah* to make me well. I recall, too, being helped down the stairs morning and evening by the women, and someone fanning me. Then the women heated bricks in the fire and tried to make me sit on them, saying that it would make me well. If I did not do as I was told, they said, I would die.

What an idea it seems, when one is scorched with fever, to add more heat to counteract the illness! Yet I suppose that there is something in this homeopathic remedy, for one reads of similar treatment in other parts of the east, and there is the tale of the African explorer whom the natives cured of smallpox by boiling him in the hollowed-out log of a tree.

My great craving all the time was for cold water, which they kept handing me. I do not know how I expressed my gratitude; but I was truly grateful for this, if not for the hot bricks.

Suddenly the fever, or whatever it was, left me. It seemed to me miraculous that I should recover in the circumstances, but it was not without after-effects, for I began to break out into terrible boils. I had been dreading something of the kind all along. How could I avoid catching some complaint in the neighbourhood of these women? It was terrible to look at their eyes, always full of matter, and apparently quite beyond a cure. Almost daily they would go through the process of doctoring each other. One would he on the floor, while another would lift up the lid of her eye, push some ointment underneath, then close the lid and stroke it round. It must have been very painful, as the patient always groaned for a time until the smart had worn off.

To continue an unpleasant subject—but it is impossible to picture my condition without allusion to such things—the boils were very large and painful, and I was in terror of getting dirt into them. When I had the chance I would tear off a piece of my muslin covering and use it as a bandage, but I dared not do this in front of the women, for I knew that the muslin would be confiscated if they saw me. There was nothing else to use; but the sores, instead of getting better, grew worse and more numerous.

The first distinct recollection which I have, after my recovery from the fever, is a visit from a man named Abdul Khalis, who spoke both English and French fluently and was very sympathetic in manner. He made a good impression on me, and I poured out my woes to him, or at least such of them as I thought it wise to tell him. It was a great relief to be able to speak to someone like this, who could understand.

Abdul Khalis told me that the townspeople of Shahraban were just as much to blame for the trouble as the tribesmen. They had known that the rising was coming and had consented to it, hoping to get their share of the plunder without any of the blame. He was an ex-Turkish officer and knew the Arabs well. He assured me I would not be killed, because they thought that, when the British came and were told that I had received protection in the town, this would exempt them from all punishment.

He added that he had himself protested to Sheikh Majid about my treatment; but this unfortunately had the effect of making it more difficult for him to visit me, as the Arabs feared that he would try to do too much for me. When I asked him why my *Sahib* had been killed, he said the rising had not been against individuals but against the government and their administration. Before he went, he said that his mother and sister, with whom he lived, would send me any little things I wanted; and he promised to get me some black material to make clothes. I thanked him, but of course did not attach much importance to the promise, as I was only too used to being told that 'it will be brought.' When nothing arrived for a few days, I simply thought that the promise of Abdul Khalis was worth as much as those of my captors.

Sheikh Majid would occasionally send for me to go to the men's quarters. At these times there was always a large assembly of men present. I do not know why they sent for me, as it was seldom there were any questions of importance. Hamid explained that it was better for me to go to the men, as some of them, being strangers and not relatives, could not easily come to the women's quarters. These visits varied the monotony of my existence. The big front door was left open, and one could see the people passing outside and occasional horsemen galloping by. The latter were a source of terror to me, and I could not resist jumping up and running out of sight if they stooped to look in through the door. In spite of all the assurances which I had had, I could not get rid of the obsessing thought of being killed.

There was one pleasant feature in connection with the visits to the men's quarters—the coffee. There was always a liberal supply. Though only a tiny drop was poured out into a very small china bowl, it was so strong and delicious that one mouthful would have been enough in an ordinary way. But I always returned my cup for more twice and sometimes thrice. After I had finished, the same cup was refilled and handed to the others. I was glad that the coffee was always offered to me first!

Once, on one of these visits, I had a great fright. I was sitting next to Sheikh Hassan, who was trying to open a tin of cigarettes. He drew his dagger with such a flourish that I sprang up and ran away from him. A peal of laughter greeted this; but my nerves were too unstrung to see the joke. Sheikh Majid told me to sit down, there was nothing to fear, and Hassan finished opening the tin with his dagger farther away from me.

During these visits of mine to the men's quarters, the women were always looking through the peep-holes of the courtyard door or through the narrow slits in the wall of their roof, through which they could see without being seen. I used to wonder whether it annoyed them to watch me sitting among their men, when they themselves could not go past them unveiled!

Then one day I was summoned to the men's quarters, and found assembled there the Indians who were prisoners in Sheikh Majid's house, together with two others, Mr. Thomas and Mr. Dean. The latter were subordinates of the Political Staff, and were both Christians, and, when they escaped from the Qeshlah, had been taken to the house of a certain Hassan Agha Zingana. This was where Iskender was also staying. He was now with them, and when I arrived told me that the Arabs had decided to send us all to Beled Ruz. He advised me to say I did not want to go.

All the chief men of Shahraban were there, and a discussion went on for a very long time. It seemed very difficult for them to make up their minds. At last, however, it was settled that we should all be sent to Beled Ruz in *arabanas*—a kind of conveyance more Like our brick-cart than anything else. I was indignant, and told Sheikh Majid that it was absurd to think of sending me to live in the company of all these Indians. I was an Englishwoman, and it would be an unheard-of thing to despatch me to a strange place with natives whom I hardly knew at all.

I protested long and earnestly. Mr. Dean suggested that I should speak to Hassan Agha Zingana, and tell him that my health made it impossible for me to stand the journey. Hassan Agha, he said, was a much bigger man than Sheikh Majid in Shahraban, and if he said I was not to go all would be well. I spoke to Hassan Agha, and explained how ill I was, and declared that I would not willingly leave this house.

Of course, it was not that I wanted to stop at Sheikh Majid's. But the idea of that horrible journey of about twenty-five miles in an *arabana*, under a glaring sun, with no *topee* to protect me, and the thought of the possibility of being attacked on the way—I could not put much trust in Sheikh Majid's guarantee against attack—were appalling. And then, at the end of the journey, was I to be herded with the Indians, compelled to eat with them, and to have no privacy for an indefinite period? No one knew where the British were, nor what likelihood there was of any rescue. What little hope we had was based on nothing substantial.

Hassan Agha listened to me, and another long debate ensued between him and Sheikh Majid. Finally, Hassan Agha said that I should not be sent away with the others. I was relieved, although I felt in a way that the presence of these others had been a certain protection, and now I was being left behind alone, except for Baines, who was too ill to do anything.

I went back to the women's quarters and up to the roof. The women talked a great deal about the journey to Beled Ruz, and as far as I could m.ake out, it was going to be very far from a pleasant one, so that I was evidently well out of it.

That night there was continual firing for about three hours. I got up and made Jumeila give me one of the women's *abbas*, which I wrapt closely round me, keeping my face covered. Then I lay down beside her. The women did not appear to worry very much about the firing. Perhaps they had been warned to expect it. With me it was different. I was extremely thankful when the shots sounded farther away and at last ceased entirely. I stopped with Jumeila, however, expecting firing to begin again at close quarters, and only in the early morning did I return to my own bed.

When Gosdan arrived with my tea, he said that they had all started for Beled Ruz before sunrise, including the sergeant.

'Not the sergeant!' I exclaimed. 'I thought he was much too ill to be moved. He will never get through the journey. The first jolting of the *arabana* will knock him up.'

But Gosdan said he had gone nevertheless. 'Nobody left, *Memsahib*, but you and me.'

So *now* I was left all alone! How easy it would be to kill me now and say that I had died of fever! I told Gosdan this; but he would not have it. He was sure they were not going to kill me. Besides, he was at hand and, if he heard me call, he would come and stand by me. They would have to kill him too.

I told him to do nothing of the kind, but to keep out of the way. Really this boy's pluck was admirable. He never seemed to know what fear was. I wished that I could be like him in this respect; and, as a matter of fact, he did seem always to inspire some courage in me. I thought to myself that, if an Armenian boy can face death as bravely as this, it will not do for me, an Englishwoman, to exhibit cowardice.

Still, I did not find it easy to avoid feeling a coward at the moment. The others were all gone, and what prospect was there for me? The thought of escape was madness. To slip away at night and try to walk to Baqubah was impossible. I should only lose my way a few miles out of Shahraban, and either be stricken down by the sun or else be captured by a worse tribe than those I was with. It was no use thinking of getting away on horseback, either. Even if I succeeded in getting down from the roof at night, I should be heard taking the horse out of the stable and through the women's quarters. At the back of all was the thought that I was a woman. It is bad enough for a man to attempt escape, with the knowledge that if he is recaptured he will be shot. How much worse for a woman, who may have to face a hundred unknown terrors.

Later Hamid came and told me that the sergeant had been brought back to the house. He had got as far as the gates of the town, but had been too ill to proceed farther, so had been allowed to return. When I asked if I could see him Hamid said, 'Later, sister, he is in pain and very bad now.' I asked other questions, but Hamid would not venture beyond 'I don't know, sister,' in reply.

In the evening I succeeded in seeing Baines. He was alone in his room, and the courtyard was very deserted. Hamid, of course, was with us all the time. Baines described to me how they had started for the *arabanas* early that morning. He said he had walked to the *bazaar*, where they were to collect, but his wounds hurt him very much during the walk. When he got into an *arabana* and sat down on the wooden floor, it began to jolt violently over the appalling roads, and the pain was intense. The cart was stopped, and a bundle of straw put down for him to sit on. But it was no good. The Arabs realised that he could not attempt the journey. When they reached the gates near the Qeshlah he was thoroughly done up. Some townspeople lifted him out and carried him back to Sheikh Majid's house. He hoped he would not be moved again, he said, until the British came.

The doctor now arrived to dress his wounds, and I left, quite convinced that Baines would not live much longer, so ill and thin he looked.

The following day there was no food provided of any description, and all I had was a cup of tea in the morning. I asked Hamid and Jumeila and others of the women for something to eat; but, though some of them went as if to fetch it, nothing arrived. I saw Baines again in the evening, and found that he too had befell left without food and was very hungry. We both wondered what this meant. I asked for Sheikh Majid, for I thought he could scarcely refuse to provide anything; but was told that he was not in the house. So there was nothing to do but go to bed hungry.

When Gosdan brought my early tea next morning, I inquired why there had been no food the day before. He did not know, and as far as I could make out there was no food for this day either. By midday nothing appeared, and when I asked if I might have an egg, I was told there were none—though the courtyard was swarming with chickens. By this time I was feeling faint with hunger: for I had more appetite since the fever had left me. What did it mean? Was this some new treatment which they had devised for us, and how long were they going to keep it up?

In the evening I heard that Sheikh Majid had returned. I asked to see him, and he paid me a visit. When I told him that I was hungry, and might I have something to eat, he professed to be very surprised. But I believe that it was by his orders all the time that we had been starved. He promised that coffee should be sent. This turned up in about an hour's time, and then Jassim came in with a few dates which I ate up quickly, hoping something else would follow. Nothing more came, but at least the edge was taken off my hunger, and I felt better.

Two days without food may sound a very short time; but when it is actually *you* who are hungry it seems ages!

It was soon after this, perhaps the next evening, that I received a summons to the men's courtyard. On my arrival there, I saw to my surprise Iskender, Mr. Thomas, and Mr. Dean.

'Why, haven't you gone to Beled Ruz? 'I exclaimed.

No, they answered, they had been left behind; and they did not seem at all pleased that I had asked the question.

Then I was told that our names and addresses were to be taken. Mr. Dean advised me not to give mine if I could help it. I did not see why not, but I presumed that he knew best. I found Abdul Khalis sitting next to me, so I asked him why they wanted these details,

MR JOHN BAINES (AS AT TIME OF FIRST PUBLICATION AND SOON AFTER RELEASE).

as they already knew my name quite well. He was not sure; perhaps they wanted the details because we were all Christians—Mr. Baines, Iskender Effendi, Mr. Thomas, Mr. Dean, Gosdan, and myself. All the Indians who were Mohammedans had been sent away, he said.

I began to think rapidly. Why were all the Christians kept in Shahraban? Was it because we were '*infidels*,' and they had decided to kill us? Then why had Baines been sent away first, and only sent back because he could not stand the journey? It was very puzzling.

The others were all talking. I asked Iskender what it was about, but he answered evasively. It is most tantalising to feel that you are being mentioned in a conversation which you are unable to follow. The few words which you catch only make you inquisitive.

At length Iskender took pencil and paper and asked my name first. Mr. Dean promptly saved me the trouble by answering, 'Mrs. Buchanan.' This somewhat annoyed me, as it had been he who advised me not to give details. When the address was asked, I simply said to Mr. Dean, 'Well, you know best,' and refused to give further information. So the address went down as 'London, England'—quite correct, but rather vague!

All in turn gave their names and addresses. I had understood them to be unwilling to do so, but now they seemed ready enough. Anyhow, I could not imagine what was the meaning of it all, and I left the men's quarters wondering.

CHAPTER 19

The First 'Fall of Baghdad'

I cannot precisely fix the day when a new terror fell upon us. It was one night, just after sunset, that a rider came up to the house and rushed in, crying, 'Baghdad has fallen, Baghdad has fallen!' Immediately there was a deafening noise. I was on the roof, and had not at first caught the announcement, and asked the women what all the noise was about; but they were far too excited themselves to pay attention to me. At last Jumeila said that the British were no longer in Baghdad.

I did not believe her, and thought I must have misunderstood what she said. I asked to see Hamid. But he, apparently, was far too busy downstairs, joining in the hubbub in the men's quarters, and no one would go to call him.

The excitement had grown tremendous, and the shouts were deafening. The women quite entered into the spirit of the thing from their own roof; and from every neighbouring house-top came cries of rejoicing and shrill screams. Visitors came in to swell the throng in the men's courtyard and add to the din.

What could it mean? This wild frenzy must be caused by some great news. At last I saw Hamid coming up our stairs, breathless. 'Baghdad has fallen,' he cried. 'The English all run away to Basrah. The tribesmen all join together and attack. The English all finished. Plenty killed.'

'Hamid!'

'Yes, all true. A rider came from Baghdad riding hard all the way to tell us.'

He could not say how many had been killed, nor whether there were any women among them. There were many questions which I wanted to ask him, but he was evidently most anxious to get away and join again in the rejoicings. I could not keep him. I did, however, ask him to get me an *abba*, and I was grateful to him for at least stopping to do this before he dashed off again to the courtyard.

I put on the *abba*, covering my face up as much as possible, and felt a Little safer. I might perhaps like this be mistaken for one of the native women.

The women on our roof were now half mad with joy, shouting to one another, uttering their war-cry, and calling down encouragement, each woman to her special man in the courtyard below. These Arab women are very martial when roused, and I believe it is their custom to follow the men when they are setting out to battle, shouting war-cries and running behind their horses, very often quite close up to danger.

Feeling utterly alone and out of it all, I went towards Jumeila, not knowing anyone else to approach. To my surprise, she pulled me closer to the wall, so that I could see over into the courtyard below. It was certainly a wonderful spectacle which met my eyes. We were in the dark, but the men's courtyard was illuminated with hurricane-lamps. In the light of these the men, having formed in as large a circle as the courtyard would permit, their swords and daggers bared and brandished high in the air, started at a run round, following each other close and shouting, 'Baghdad has fallen!' 'Hassan, Hussain!' Then they grew wilder still and began screaming at the top of their voices and discharging their rifles into the air, glancing up at their women on the roof above.

These latter were jumping up and down, waving and crying back to the men; and they were continually being reinforced by other women hurrying to see the show in Sheikh Majid's courtyard. Firing could be heard from every quarter of the town, and every housetop had its throng of yelling men, women, and children. The general excitement was far beyond anything of which Westerners are capable. All were beside themselves with frenzied joy, and I am sure that they could have done anything in such a mood.

It was a wonderful spectacle, but an appalling one, I crouched against the wall, holding on to Jumeila, while the other women all pressed close round me. At last I could bear to look no longer. Desperate fear and disgust clutched at my heart. The British had been defeated, and by a horde like this—lying, deceitful, dirty, primitive men, the very antithesis of the noble Arab whom we hear about! They were retreating, and I was left behind. For what fate?

The news so stunned me that I could not think. Luckily for me, as I now realise; for after that awful experience, which I have related, of being left alone in that little room and watched by that mysterious man, I had made a firm resolution. If necessity should arise, there was the roof and a clean sheer drop to the courtyard below. A twist as I jumped would bring me on my head, to instantaneous death. How many times at night had I woken up with a start, when some sound or a woman passing my bed had disturbed me, and sprung up, ready for that leap! Then, as the alarm proved false, I would recoil from the thought of doing what there might be no need for after all.

Now I had turned away from the mad sight below.

'Jumeila,' I said, 'I am finished.'

'No, no, don't be frightened,' she urged. 'Come!' I held on to her and looked again. The men were all rushing about and embracing one another. More lights were brought. Some threw themselves down panting and exhausted on the benches. For a short time there was a lull in the din. Then another wild group of men rushed through the door, shouting, 'Baghdad has fallen.' The other men immediately got ready to go through their war-dance again with renewed energy. They formed in a ring once more, redrew their swords, and started off again with a flourish of firing. If possible, the excitement was even madder than before. Everyone began leaping high into the air and discharging rifles until the drums of my ears seemed ready to split.

I clung tight to Jumeila and watched the door, dreading lest anyone should come through and up the stairs. No one came. I screamed at intervals, but the noise was not heard in that inferno, and no one took any notice of me.

The men at length finished their dance, and all went out into the lane in single file, singing and shooting as they went, to join the mob in the *bazaar*, there to begin their rejoicings all over again. The women were just as crazy with joy as the men, and kept up their war-cry for a long time, answering others in the distance. Finally they all sat down and talked together. I too sat down on my bed, and thought: surely this must be the end now! The British were leaving the country post-haste, and what reason had my captors for keeping me alive now? Absolutely none that I could see.

I went over to Jumeila and said, 'When the men come back, will they kill me?' All the women laughed, as if they considered my question very funny.

'No, no,' they said, 'this is Sheikh Majid's house, and now you stay here for always.'

My heart sank still lower. I felt I would rather face death now than end my days here. But I did not believe what they said. I was sure that, now the British had been defeated and were retreating, it was most unlikely the Arabs would keep me here with them, a useless woman and to them an *infidel*. Yes, death must be near now. I was determined not to scream when the men came up for me. It would be soon over, I kept telling myself. I thought of the way in which Billy had died, fearless and unflinching to the very end. How wonderful they had all been, indeed. I must imitate their example. After all, I had a lot to be grateful for. My little John was safe, and under the best possible care.

I wanted to pray and tried to, but I could not concentrate. All sorts of reminiscences kept crowding on my mind, little things that at the time had passed almost unnoticed, but now were very clear. One incident stood out most vividly. We had been going for a ride one evening. I was just coming downstairs when Billy called, 'Ready, sweetheart?' I answered, 'Coming,' and he ran up the stairs, and we met half-way and kissed. Perhaps now he was waiting for me and asking if I was ready, and we should soon meet in a place where no terror was.

★★★★★★

How I lived through the next day I do not know. The state of my nerves was terrible. Every hour was spent in anticipation of that shot or sword-thrust which was to cut life short. The waiting was dreadful, far worse, it seemed to me, than the reality could have been, had the end come. This was the first day that I was left entirely alone and unwatched, which was in itself a very bad sign. It confirmed me in the belief that Baghdad had fallen. They had no fear of my escaping now. There was nowhere for me to go.

I asked for Hamid several times, and at last he came. He gave a graphic account of the fall of the city. The British had 'run away,' fighting as they went. I knew that the 'running away' could not be true. I had seen, only so lately, how our men stand unwavering against overwhelming odds. Then Hamid said how pleased everyone was now that the British were gone. The Arabs had never liked us, and our ways did not suit them. I was very indignant, knowing how many valuable lives had been lost by us, and how much money had been spent on this country. It was disgusting to hear that we were not wanted and had been turned out. I dared not protest too much; but I reminded the boy how much we had done for the Arabs. 'We manage all the time without you before,' he replied, 'now we manage much better.'

133

It was useless to argue further. I asked him if I might have a pencil and some paper. 'What for, sister?'

'To draw pictures with,' was all I could think of to say.

Hamid looked at me. 'You very ill, sister,' he said. 'The women all say if you don't get better you die.'

I believe that Hamid thought I was a little bit mad to want to draw pictures at a time Like this: but he brought me a pencil and some paper, which happened to be one of Baines's account-books. I was very pleased, but dared not show it. Opening a page at random, I began drawing. The moment he had gone, I turned to a fresh page and began:

To be given to Mrs. Buchanan

(address)

Then I wrote as swiftly as I could, telling my husband's mother how all had happened, and how wonderful her son had been, and ask-ing that little John should be brought up to be as fearless as his father. I told her that if she ever got this note she would know that I had been shot after the fall of Baghdad.

It was not a very long letter, but it gave the incidents of the tragedy at the Qeshlah. I do not quite know why I wrote it, or what prospects I thought there were of Mrs. Buchanan ever getting it. But I hoped that, if the British did return and by any chance came to this house, they might discover it. I tore the page out of the book, folded it, put it in my dress, and went to the stable. There I hunted for a long time for a suitable hiding-place. In among the straw, with one corner sticking out, it would have been noticed at once by the Arabs, or if overlooked by them would have been lost when the straw was moved or trampled underfoot by the horses. I decided at last to put it in one of the many cracks and gaps in the walls, where the heat had dried the mud. I fixed it in one of these, pushing it in until almost out of sight.

I felt happier after this, and trusted that my message would reach its destination if anything happened to me. When I returned to my room, I began another letter of the same type, which I meant to give to Baines, so that if he survived me and ultimately got away from Shahraban, he might be able to deliver it. I had only got half-way through the second letter when Hamid returned. Immediately I went back to the page with my drawing on it and began adding to it. But Hamid asked for the pencil, and when I begged him to let me finish he sat down and waited. Then he took the pencil, so that was the end of my writing for the day, but he left me the book, which I put on the little ledge in my room.

I could not see Baines until the following day. I was going to give him what I had written and ask him to keep it on him, so that if anything happened to me and he should reach England, he might deliver the message. But I had forgotten that his hands were useless still, and that if he wanted to get at his pockets he had to ask someone else to do it for him. He could not conceal the letter on him. We decided, therefore, that it was best to leave it in the book, and if luck favoured him he would get the book when (and if) the British came. I put it underneath some old things and oddments on the ledge and left it there unnoticed.

I begged Baines, if I was killed and he ever got away and back to England, to tell my relatives everything. Somehow I was just as convinced that he would not be killed as I was that I should—which was foolish, because the Arabs would naturally kill him too if they killed me. He was very cheering and hopeful. If Baghdad had fallen, which he very much doubted, the British would never evacuate the country like this. Think of the effect on India! Troops would be sent out at once from England to Basrah, and other troops from India must have started already, as soon as they heard of the trouble. In the end we should be rescued, though now it might take time.

His visit had its usual tonic effect on me. The picture he drew of the state of affairs was very rosy in comparison with mine, and he infected me with some of his hopefulness.

About this time there was a large gathering of notables in Sheikh Majid's house, to discuss who should be chief Sheikh of Shahraban. The noise they made was terrific, and though they met three times no decision was ever arrived at. The position was left as it was, with no acknowledged chief, though many considered themselves qualified for the post.

There was now much talk about 'the Turks,' and I asked Hamid what was being said. He explained that now the British were all gone, the Turks were advancing. They were already at Quizil Robat, and would soon be in Shahraban. When I asked him what would happen to me then, he said they would take me away as their prisoner. Everybody in Shahraban, he added, would be very pleased at their coming, as the Turks understood the Arabs, and had much better ways for them than the British.

Later, when I heard the sound of aeroplanes overhead, someone

135

ran in, excitedly crying that they were Turkish aeroplanes. The women were all out in the courtyard looking up. After my last experience in connection with the British plane, I took no interest in these.

When I saw Gosdan next I asked him how the Turks treated their prisoners. Were they good, like the British, or did they kill the women? To my surprise, he said that the Turks were very good to their prisoners. His own brother had been captive with them for eighteen months, and all the time 'plenty to eat, plenty cigarettes, no work'—a very different tale from what we were generally given to understand. And yet Gosdan was an Armenian! 'No fear, *Memsahib*,' he concluded, 'if they take you, much better for you than here.'

When I saw him next, Gosdan gave me a terrible shock and quite undid the good which my visit from Baines had done me. Had he heard anything fresh, I asked him. 'Yes, *Memsahib*,' he answered, 'they come to me today and say Madam killed tribesmen at the fight at the Qeshlah.'

'Gosdan!' I shrieked. 'What did you say?'

'I say, "Yes," *Memsahib*.'

'How mad of you! Why didn't you say I did not?'

'You tell me always speak the truth, much better.'

Yes; but didn't he realise that we were prisoners, I demanded, and must be most careful what we said? Who had asked him the question?

Three men had come and asked him, he replied. He did not know who they were.

I besought him never to do such a thing again. I thought he had more sense. If he were asked again, he must deny it. He must come back soon and tell me everything else he heard.

Gosdan went away quite crestfallen. Apparently he had not at all realised that he had signed my death-warrant. Now they knew *that*, what chance had I? I had thought that, as so many days had elapsed since the 13th and they had never spoken of it, no one knew.

That night I slept with my head thrown back. 'Let them kill me swiftly, in my sleep!' was my prayer.

CHAPTER 20

A Feast; and an Assassin

One morning about this time preparations were obviously being made very early for some great feast. First of all, the courtyard was put in a state of comparative neatness, my room was swept, and the mattresses were stacked more tidily than usual. Then little Leg-Leg, Keremah's daughter, had a bath, a proceeding which she hated; but afterwards new clothes were put on her, and her delight was unbounded. She had a bright blue-coloured frock, with lines of lace down it—I recognised from where the lace had come! Leg-Leg ran about holding out her frock for the admiration of other little girls and boys who came in that day, all in brightly coloured *abbas* and looking much cleaner than was their wont. All the children had their pockets full of dried melon-pips, which they continually cracked and ate.

In our courtyard there was a great display of these melon-pips, whole heaps being brought in and fried, then laid on a slab in the sun to dry again. Meanwhile Keremah was busy kneading a huge bowl of dough for making cakes. When I could get hold of Hamid, I asked him what these preparations were for. 'It is our New Year,' he replied, 'a very big day. The women make plenty cakes and eat them, and all very happy.'

I could see the preparations for the 'plenty cakes,' but I cannot say that I noticed much of the 'all very happy' among the women so far. They all went about their work as usual, like dumb, driven animals, seeming to take very little interest in it.

In the afternoon mattresses were spread out on the floor of the room I called mine, my bed being pushed into a corner, as far out of the way as possible. Numbers of women-friends came to the house, making quite a large party when all had arrived. Everyone was wearing her best clothes. Some of them on entering kissed Jumeila. Others began to *salaam* her; but she would not allow this, and made every one kiss her. The amount of kissing that went on at the arrival of each new guest was tremendous!

I particularly noticed one girl who came to the festival. I had never seen her before. Her forehead and chin were heavily tattooed, but she was very handsome, and her hair was wonderful, falling in two long plaits over her shoulders to below her knees; it must have reached the ground when it was loose. All the Arab women have two long plaits to their waists, but I had never seen hair like this before, and it was untouched by henna.

The elder women had brought their spinning with them, the younger married ones were occupied with their babies. They seated themselves on mattresses, and cigarettes were handed round. I noticed that a great number of them had some of my finery on. One woman, in particular, evidently had an undergarment of mine, as she took great pains to show it to the other women, and equally great pains to prevent my even so much as getting a glimpse of it; but, strangely enough, this failed to annoy me. I suppose my spirit was too much crushed by now.

Next came the making of the cakes. A huge slab of tin was brought in. The dough was pulled off in pieces and rolled into little balls, which were passed on to be patted out flat, and then crossed many times with a knife. A number of the visitors assisted in the work, remixing the dough and rolling the balls. When the slab was covered with round flat cakes, it was taken out into the courtyard and put over a fire. The cakes were turned until done, and were then brought back and handed round and eaten hot. They looked very nice; but none was offered to me, though there were plenty to spare. An *infidel*, I presumed, must not have any. A great bowl of melon-pips followed, and the women spent the rest of their time eating these. This was a slow process, for each one was cracked with the teeth before the tiny kernel was eaten.

Sheikh Hassan came in to speak to his wife, whereon all the women quickly drew their *abbas* across their faces. Keremah went up to him, and pushed him away from the room, rating him soundly. There was much giggling among the women over this.

At last, when the room was hazy with smoke and stiflingly hot, the visitors began to go. I was exceedingly thankful, for they seemed to have been there hours, and my head was buzzing.

In the evening a big meal was prepared for the men. A great deal of cooking was done, principally by Jumeila. It appeared that the re-

138

sult was not as pleasing to Sheikh Majid as it should have been, for later he came in and had a quarrel with his daughter. They shouted at each other for quite half an hour. Certainly Jumeila must have had the best of the argument, for she followed her father finally to the gate between the two courtyards, going for him all the time, while he was scarcely answering her back. Then she returned and told the other women what she thought of the quarrel—and also her opinion of her father, which I gathered was not exactly what one would term filial respect!

During the evening Hamid came to me with a parcel, and said, 'From Abdul Khalis Effendi.' I took it eagerly and unrolled it. At last a promise had been kept to send me some clothes. But, to my disappointment, the clothes consisted only of a piece of bright pink stuff and another piece of black material, not enough to make a frock. However, there was some compensation in a cake of scented soap, a reel of black cotton, and a needle. I was very pleased with these, especially with the soap. I told Hamid to thank Abdul Khalis very much, and asked if he would come and see me if he could.

When Abdul Khalis came I thanked him again, but hinted at the insufficiency of the 'clothes' he had sent. He suggested that the black material would make an excellent short coat. I didn't want a coat, I said; but he persisted that all English ladies wore them. Then I told him how much I should like some black silk such as the Arab women's *abbas* were made of, for a dress. This, it appeared, was not to be had in Shahraban, all the women sending to Baghdad for such stuff, but he promised to bring a man from the *bazaar* with some rolls of material from which to choose. He said I could take sufficient to make myself a dress.

One more request I had to make. Was it possible for him to procure me a toothbrush? He thought his sister had one which she could send me. I cannot say that the idea of a second-hand toothbrush appealed to me; but it would be better than nothing!

I had not seen Abdul Khalis since the reported fall of Baghdad, so I asked him if he had heard of it. Yes, he said, but he did not put much faith in the report. The Shahraban people were ready to believe any good news. He thought that it would have been impossible for the British to have evacuated Baghdad as easily as they were supposed to have done, with all their guns, armoured cars, and aeroplanes. I spoke of the aeroplane we had seen at the Qeshlah, which had never returned. He seemed very surprised, and said he could not understand it.

He told me that the tribesmen were growing very strong, and there was a possibility of their breaking into Shahraban. If it was suggested that I should be moved from Sheikh Majid's house, he advised me to refuse to go unless I was to be moved to the house of another sheikh.

If Baghdad had really fallen, I asked, and the tribesmen were to break into Shahraban, would I be killed? Perhaps I should, he admitted, if the British had gone; but he did not believe they had. This was rather mixed comfort.

As he was leaving, Abdul Khalis said that his mother wanted to send me food, but Sheikh Majid would not allow this, saying that I always had plenty.

'You know that is not true,' I replied indignantly.

'Yes, but I can do nothing.' He seemed genuinely sorry, and came again later with a man, bringing rolls of stuff from the *bazaar*. There was nothing I liked, for everything was of cotton. However, I chose one piece, and had enough measured off to make a dress. Directly Abdul Khalis had gone I remembered that I had no scissors. Also, someone had taken my needle and cotton and the piece of pink material. So I was in exactly the same predicament as before. When I asked Jumeila for scissors, needle, and cotton, she said that there were no such things in the house.

I think that it must have been the same evening, not very late, that I was summoned to the men's quarters. On arriving there I found Sheikh Majid, Abdul Khalis, and a number of the townspeople. I could see no sign of Baines. I sat between the *sheikh* and Abdul Khalis, unable to follow the conversation, except that I could make out that there was a lot being said about the Turks.

Suddenly a man galloped up to the door, leapt off his horse, and came in, the horse following him. 'Baghdad has fallen! Baghdad has fallen!' he shouted.

I turned at once to Abdul Khalis and asked him if it could be true this time.

He was still incredulous. I was very alarmed and begged Sheikh Majid to let me go, but he said it was better for me to stay there. Trembling with fear, I remained where I was. The excitement grew fast. Then some of the men shouted and drew their swords. Someone fired a shot into the air. Screaming, I sprang up, and the next moment was running for dear life up the stairs to the women's roof. There was no one there. Night had not yet fallen, and it was still possible to see, but I crouched against the further wall, absolutely terrified. The noise grew louder and louder in the courtyard below. There was a clashing of steel mingled with the wild cries and the sound of neighbours rushing in to join in the hubbub.

I could tell that the same frenzied scene was coming all over again which I had witnessed when the fall of Baghdad was reported before. I had not the strength, however, to look over the wall or through the slits, even if I had had the desire to do so. I could not move from where I was.

None of the women came up to the roof. Presumably they had a good view from the door of the courtyard and took their share of the proceedings from their own quarters.

I was still crouching against the further wall when I saw slowly come up over the wall from the men's side a head and the end of a rifle-muzzle. My heart seemed to stop beating. I watched, fascinated with sheer terror, as the apparition continued to rise until the rifle was level with the top of the wall and a man's head and shoulders were visible. His eyes were looking straight at me. I could just make out his features in the fading light. It was Mohamed, the son of Barkah, a man whom I had always hated. Every nerve in my body grew tense, and I slowly pulled myself down until I was almost on the floor of the roof.

A shot rang out. . . . Dry mud from the wall, about a foot above, spattered all over me. I sank in a heap.

Immediately the man sprang up on the wall, gave a shout, waved his rifle in the air, and rushed off down to rejoin the others.

Far too unnerved to stir, I lay prostrate on the roof, crying and asking myself again and again, 'Why isn't it all over?'

It was a long time before the men went out of their courtyard and the women came up to the roof. They found me still lying in a heap on the floor. When I told them that I had been shot at and begged that it might be finished now, they declined to believe anyone had shot at me.

I clung close to Jumeila, refusing to leave her, and lay down on her mattress, getting the others to sit round. If another shot were fired at me now, it would hit one of their own women—and I knew they would never do that.

All that night I lay by Jumeila on her mattress. The shouting and sound of rifle-shots continued far into the night.

CHAPTER 21

I Leave the Harem

After this second 'fall of Baghdad' I was left to my own resources practically all the time. No one took any notice of me, or attempted to watch or follow me about. In a way it was a relief—especially after the last example of somebody taking an interest in my whereabouts, on that evening on the roof of the women's quarters! Yet I was made to realise, in a very uncomfortable way, what this neglect meant. Food was only brought to me after I had asked many times for something to eat; and then the only meal I could ever get was a round of bread and raw tomatoes. I still had, it is true, the tea which was purchased out of the daily dole of one *rupee* four *annas*. But for anything more solid there was only this bread and tomatoes. Imagine Arab bread and raw tomatoes for any one in my state of health! I must indeed have had an iron constitution to begin with, to endure this diet and be alive at the end of it. Had I not originally been in perfect health, I could never have survived the awful horrors and hardships of my captivity.

The thought that I was doomed to remain in this house for an indefinite period made the hours crawl along. If only I had had something to distract my mind from the all-absorbing thought of violent death it would have been different, but there was nothing; and the hope, however faint, of a rescue had faded away entirely.

There was once a diversion, but not of a kind to make my thoughts dwell less on death. A great commotion arose of a sudden on a neighbouring roof, and men and women could be heard shouting at the tops of their voices. Down in the street others were yelling too, and there was a great banging on a door. I felt sure at first that someone was going to be murdered; and what seemed most likely was that the people in the street were after me and had gone to the wrong house. I asked Hamid, as soon as I could see him, what the disturbance meant.

One of the townspeople, he told me, had killed a tribesman during a quarrel over the loot at the Qeshlah, and now the dead man's people were demanding blood-money.

The *Koran*, Hamid explained, allowed the heirs of the murdered man to accept money-compensation out of the property of the murderer, instead of their being bound to kill him in his turn.

At last something happened to break the long series of days without a name or date, and to restore me to a sense of the calendar. I had long ceased, as I have explained, to distinguish days except by their events; and what can bring home to us more clearly than that the feeling of being cut off from the outside world?

Well, one morning Sheikh Hassan came up on the women's roof, and told me to be quick and get ready, as I was to be moved to another house. 'To whose house?' I asked.

'To Hassan Agha Zingana's,' he replied. I inquired why; but the *sheikh* merely said that it had been decided, and I must go.

I recalled what Abdul Khalis had told me, and was determined not to leave unless I was absolutely forced. I was much too ill to go out into the streets, I said. I could not bear again the scenes I had gone through on the visit to my billet.

Sheikh Hassan seemed very annoyed with me, and went out obviously angry. He returned with Sheikh Majid and Iskender. The latter told me to get ready at once, for we were going to be sent to another house. I renewed my protest to him, but he said there was nothing to be done. I must go. He, the Sergeant, Thomas, and Dean were going too.

Having made every possible excuse, I was at length compelled to give way. There was obviously, as Iskender said, nothing to be done. So I asked them to leave me while I got ready. The *sheikhs* were plainly very loath to leave, but as I refused to stir till they went, they eventually left me. I washed and did my hair. Sheikh Hassan, to my great annoyance, kept coming back in the midst of my toilet to see that I was getting on and to adjure me to hurry. This, together with my terrible feeling of illness, made me slower than ever.

When I was nearly ready I called to Jumeila to come up, and asked her if I could take the face flannel with me, having nothing else with which to wash. She said no, it belonged to the household, and all the women used it! After that I had no desire to take it! I had never seen the women wash, but I suppose that they must have gone through this ceremony on special occasions. No wonder, then, that I had broken out into those awful running sores, if I had been using the same flannel as they!

I inquired of Jumeila why I was being sent away. She did not know and called Hamid, who professed equal ignorance. It was better for the Christians to be together, he suggested.

'Does that mean that we are all going to be killed?'

'I don't know, sister. The tribesmen getting very strong and wanting to come into Shahraban.'

Then he said something to the effect that it would be bad if we were killed in anybody's house—which seemed to imply that if we were killed in an empty house it would be nobody's business!

'But we are going to Hassan Agha Zingana's,' I objected.

'No, sister, you are all going to the school.'

'What? I alone with the Indians? Hamid, it is preposterous. I am an English woman. I can't be sent to live with those Indians, as if I were a man. Tell Sheikh Majid to come.'

The *sheikh* came, and Hamid explained what I had said. But he was quite firm. I *was* going, and I must hurry as the others were waiting. He would take me himself, however, to see that I was quite safe.

The prospect was awful of going out through those streets again, and at the end of the journey being shut up with the Indian prisoners. How could I face it? But there was no alternative. Sheikh Majid was evidently in no mood to be trifled with, so I finished my preparations, crying all the time.

Then I asked Jumeila if I could take the camp- bed and pillow and muslin covering with me. The bed and pillow, she answered, but not the muslin; that belonged to the women.

Mr. Baines, Iskender Effendi, Mr. Thomas, and Mr. Dean were waiting for me. I was glad to see that Baines was one of the party. Here at least was one Englishman, whom I knew. The others, apart from Iskender, were known to me only by sight. I spoke to Baines at once.

'Where are we going? Are we going to be killed?'

'No, we'll be all right. Try not to think of death so much.'

I begged him not to leave me, and to see that I was not taken away from the place where he was. We were the only English people, and we must keep together.

He looked no better than when I last had seen him, but he kept up his old cheerfulness and courage. He would see that I was not sent away alone, he promised; and he told me not to be frightened as we went through the *bazaar*. We were sure to be quite safe, for Sheikh

Hamid was in Shahraban now.

He pointed out that there would at least be one advantage in the move, that we should be able to talk more freely; and altogether he succeeded in putting a little spirit into me, for which I was very grateful. I needed it badly.

We started off. It was a ghastly journey through the town and part of the *bazaar*. Crowds flocked round us. I kept screaming all the time. Sheikh Majid was dashing about with his stick, striking at the mob to keep them off. The other prisoners walked in a ring, with me in the centre and Gosdan right on the edge, fearless as usual. All of them constantly assured me that it was all right and that, though so many of the men carried arms, none would use them.

At last we came to the school, which was a house used as a school for the children of Shahraban. It was a dreary-looking place, nothing but three rooms with benches in them, a courtyard, and a roof. The moment I got in and away from the crowd, I lay down on a bench, feeling very ill and sick. Sheikh Majid and some other notables of the town came in and sat down. I had to get up and go out into the courtyard, where I was violently sick. To my great surprise, Iskender came out and held my head, while Mr. Thomas brought me some water in an old jam-tin—the only receptacle that could be found in the place.

I felt very grateful, if somewhat embarrassed, at these two men looking after me like this. It was indeed a change after my recent experiences. They found a mattress from somewhere and made me lie down, and someone brought me some grapes. All seemed very worried and kept asking me if I wanted anything. I gradually revived, and when the Arabs had gone was able to join in the talk. What a blessing it was to be able to talk in English all the time and to be understood!

We looked about the house and could discover only one hiding-place in case of danger. That was a big niche high up in the wall, with just room enough for one person. By their glances I could tell that they destined this for me if the need should arise.

Some more townspeople arrived, none of whom I had ever seen before. One was a man named Ali, who came with his brother. The latter told Iskender that he had rescued me from the ditch after the fall of the Qeshlah. Iskender repeated this to me. I had no recollection of the man's face, and told Iskender so. 'Well, say you do and thank him,' he replied. 'His brother is a very big man among the townspeople.' So I smiled and expressed my gratitude, at which the Arab fidgeted and seemed very embarrassed.

We had now plenty of grapes, and several of the men brought cigarettes. I saw that at any rate there would be better cheer than at Sheikh Majid's. With the arrival of my camp-bed, which was taken up to the roof, I felt almost reconciled to the school.

In the evening Sheikh Majid came back, with Sheikh Hamid. The conversation was very strained until the former left, and after his departure some of us expressed our opinions of him pretty freely. Sheikh Hamid stayed and looked over the school. He said that we could not be left here, as it was not at all a safe place to put us in, the roof being in full view of the bazaar, without even a low wall on that side as a protection, and declared that he would come back himself in the morning and take us to a better and safer billet.

I was very relieved at this, for I did not at all care for the proximity of the *bazaar* with our exposed roof and only a very feeble street-door. The idea of facing the streets again next day was not pleasant; but then there would be Sheikh Hamid to escort us. It may seem strange that this man's presence should have inspired me with comfort, knowing that it was his tribesmen who were responsible for so much. It was a fact, however, that, all the time my nerves were strung up and my body tense in expectation of death, the moment he entered I would relax. Respecting my horror of firearms, he never carried any when I was there. Then his movements were slow, and his voice lower and quieter than the rest. He never shouted, and when the others all shouted and became excited over a discussion, he merely raised his hand and said 'Majid,' or the name of whoever else it was who was most violent. Immediately a silence would fall, or at least a comparative silence. Most certainly this *sheikh* of the Beni Tamim was the Arab I liked best of any I had come across since my captivity began.

When he departed, two guards were left behind to protect us. They were exceedingly fierce-looking men, and their rifles never quitted their hands for an instant. Though my fellow-prisoners assured me that the guards were all right, and that they would not use their rifles against me, I did not at all relish the company of these two Arabs.

We sat in the courtyard talking for some time. I discovered that this day was the 28th of August—fifteen days since that awful nightmare at the Qeshlah. The Indians had fortunately been able to keep count of the days, so that now at last I felt I knew where I was. Then the question arose, where was I to sleep? Of course it must be on the roof, for the heat in the courtyard would be intolerable. But where could the men sleep in that case? I realised that it would be far too selfish of me to expect them to stay downstairs while I monopolised the roof. I had lived too near 'the shadow of death' during the last days to think of the rules of propriety just then! There was nothing for it but that all should sleep on the roof. The sentries remained downstairs.

That night was a ghastly one. All through the long hours the *bazaar* was humming with angry voices, and then later the people began that horrid war-dance and cry, shooting in the air all the time as they passed the part of the *bazaar* nearest the school. I was thoroughly scared, and called to the others to keep awake. Somehow the knowledge that I was not awake alone was comforting. The men, however, were all very wide-awake already, and probably, like me, none of them had been asleep. They told me that we were all right, but that it would be better for me to be on a mattress on the floor, instead of my camp-bed. Mr. Dean pulled my mattress close to the wall, and lay down himself on the edge of the roof between me and the *bazaar*. He said nothing; but I could see that he had put himself directly in the way of any bullet coming in my direction. This was a chivalrous act on his part, for only the courtyard and a narrow road divided us from the mob, and our roof must have shown distinctly in the white moonlight.

When the noise and the firing ceased I fell asleep. In the morning I awoke again to find that the others had already gone downstairs. I stayed in the shade as long as it was possible, and then went down too. Gosdan brought me some water into one of the rooms, and for the first time since my captivity I dressed alone.

Not long after Sheikh Hamid arrived, and with him his brother Sheikh Feisul, who lived in Shahraban, and some other men. They had come to take us to a new billet. I did not feel nearly so frightened going through the streets this time, and the Arabs did not swarm round us as they had always done before. They kept at a respectful distance. But how they glared at me!—at least, so I thought.

We reached at last a door some little distance from the bazaar, and not very far from Captain Wrigley's billet. Sheikh Hamid said that this was our destination. The door was opened, and we went in.

CHAPTER 22

Fellow-Prisoners

Our new prison was bare as an empty house. It had been the billet
for the A.P.O's clerks and had been completely looted. Mr. Thomas
and Mr. Dean did not seem to worry much about this. No doubt they
had been prepared to see their billet in the state we now found it.

At first I did not take in much of my surroundings. We went upstairs, and I sat down on the floor and began to cry. Though the walk
had not been long and there had been no special excitement about it,
I was tired and faint and felt desperately ill. When Iskender inquired
what was the matter, I could only beg him to get a bed or something
on which I could lie down, as I was afraid of fainting. Someone ran
downstairs at once and told one of the sentries to get a mattress. A
coffee-bench was quickly brought and put in the shade of the courtyard, and then they helped me down. I should certainly have fallen
head first if they had not done so. I lay on the bench and continued
crying. The others talked with Sheikh Hamid. I think they were all
very embarrassed and worried about me. I was not so myself, being far
too ill to care about anything.

Then the *sheikh* left, and soon after another bench arrived, with
some mattresses and quilts and my camp-bed. The Indians fixed the
bed up and put a mattress on it, and I lay down, taking little notice of
anyone or anything. At *tiffin*-time food was brought. It was no doubt
much nicer than anything I had had at Sheikh Majid's house; but
when I looked and saw a dish of rice and tomatoes, it seemed to kill
any appetite I had. Mr. Thomas put some on a plate and handed it
to me. I did not feel like food, however. Perhaps it was because I had
so little at Sheikh Majid's that now I seemed able to continue on a
starvation-diet indefinitely.

After *tiffin* the others sat on and talked. I had not even the energy

148

to listen to what they said. In the evening I felt better, and was able to go round and take note of the house. After the door through which we had entered there was a narrow passage, and then the courtyard. Leading off this, first on the left, was a room, clean but bare, with no light except what came from the open door. Next came another room, approached by some downward steps, which the Indians said no one could use. A poisonous snake had been seen in it and was supposed to live there, but had never been caught. So the 'snake-room' was uninhabitable. There was a third room, but it was very small. Upstairs there was only one room, and this was the nicest of all, as it had large spaces for windows, with wooden shutters that overhung and looked down on the street below.

The men all agreed that this upstairs room should be my 'dressing-room' for the mornings and evenings. During the afternoon it was far too hot to stay in. The large clean room downstairs, which was by far the coolest, they decided would be for me to sleep in during the afternoon, if I wished. This was their arrangement. Considering that there were only three usable rooms, I thought it more than generous. I felt how utterly selfish it would be for one woman to monopolise two rooms and four men to be herded together in one, where they could have little comfort. I told Baines that I could not consent to this; but neither he nor the others would hear of anything else. They said it was only right I should have the two rooms, and I was compelled to give way. I was truly grateful to them, and I had certainly never expected such treatment. I may add that they never grumbled at the discomfort they had to endure, and I know it must have been considerable.

After Sheikh Majid's house this privacy was glorious! Yet how I had resented the idea of being put with the men prisoners! Even in this short time I could realise how much for the better the change was, and nothing I write can ever express how highly I feel for the splendid and chivalrous way in which my fellow-prisoners behaved towards me.

Two sentries were left to guard us, as before, night and day. They carried rifles and bristled all over with ammunition. One was a most filthy, repulsive-looking creature, who inspired me with fear every time I looked at him. He had a horrid habit of standing with his hand on the hilt of his dagger, as if in readiness to draw it. The other looked less savage, but had an annoying way of always standing near us and listening, though of course he could not understand English. He did not, therefore, really interfere with the freedom of our talk, and it was a great relief to be able to speak one's own language again. Both the Indians had been educated at English schools in their country; and Iskender, as I have said before, spoke English fluently.

That evening, when the sun began to get lower, we all went on to the roof. I chose the place where I wanted my bed put, which was in the corner of the roof, as far away from the steps as possible. There were high walls—about five feet and a half—all round us, and the level of the roof was above any of the neighbouring houses, only the minaret of Shahraban being visible over the walls. When we were upstairs our supper was brought on a large round tray by one of the sentries. What it was, I do not remember; but I recollect Mr. Thomas taking out the best for me and trying to persuade me to eat. It was always Mr. Thomas who took charge of my meals.

After we had finished, we sat and talked for a long time. I kept asking my usual question, 'When are we going to be killed?' It seemed to me very curious that they had put all the Christians together, and, though the others would not admit that there was any special significance in this, I knew that they felt it was a bad sign. Before me, however, they insisted on keeping a bold front.

We discussed our treatment while we had been prisoners during the past fortnight. The Indians and Iskender told me that I had not been wise to go to Sheikh Majid's house. They had been all the time with Hassan Agha Zingana, and had been very well treated. They had had plenty of food, and indeed ate first, the household finishing the food after them. Moreover, Hassan Agha had always protected them. They told how one night, when some men had gone to the house with evil intent, he had told them that they should only enter over his dead body. As I heard them talk, I bitterly regretted that I had not remembered Hassan Agha's name that day when I was taken prisoner. Wrigley, Billy, and I had dined with him one night before the trouble, and he had prepared a wonderful meal for us. Had I only had the sense to think of him, I should have been spared all those awful days at Sheikh Majid's.

They were all quite sure that Baghdad had not really fallen, and were confident that troops were already on their way to rescue us, but which way, down from the Persian side or up from Baghdad, they could not say. To ease my mind, no doubt, they professed their belief that they were coming from both sides. Mr. Thomas had an idea that we would be rescued on the 8th of September. Why he selected that day I do not know, but he stuck to it firmly, and was so certain that he succeeded in convincing me, and I began to count the days. It was now the 29th of August; and so there were only ten more days before we should be free!

The guards had come up to the roof with us, and were listening to all we said. As they could not understand, this did not matter much. We avoided names as much as possible, or disguised them. Sheikh Majid, for instance, became 'Two-face.' Iskender said that he was a thoroughly dangerous man, before whom one must be very careful what one said. This made me feel very glad indeed to be out of his house.

That night I slept in the corner of the roof, the men on the other side, between me and the sentries. But in spite of this, I could not get to sleep for a long time, constantly expecting to see one of the Arabs steal across the roof and spring at me; and when at last I fell off it was only to have a violent nightmare, out of which Mr. Dean mercifully awoke me by asking what was the matter. I had been groaning and making such weird noises that I had alarmed the others.

On the following day Sheikh Hamid came to see if we were comfortable. I for one could certainly say that I was far more comfortable than I had ever been since I had fallen into Arab hands. He suggested that, if I liked, I should go to another house, where I could be alone. He would put sentries to guard me, he said. But the idea of being alone in a house, with Arab sentries as 'protectors,' was too much for me. I answered at once that I would rather remain where I was, in the company of Mr. Baines and the other prisoners.

He also suggested that it would be better for us to go to Beled Ruz. It would be all right for me, he said, as his womenfolk were there, and they would look after me. At first we all liked the idea, and after the *sheikh* had left, we practically decided we would go. Iskender, in particular, was most anxious about it. He had some wonderful scheme of escaping to Baghdad from that point, but on the following day Baines and the Indians advised me that it was much better to stay where we were. There were the dangers on the road to be considered. If Iskender was so keen on going, he could go alone, they said. I made up my mind to stay; and finally Iskender decided to stay too.

Before we left. Sheikh Hamid promised that we should each have one rupee four *annas* a day; and now it was paid regularly, which made a great difference. He told me to ask for what food I liked. I said I should like some chicken-broth—never expecting that it would come. But it did, the very same day, and two or three times afterwards.

We had numerous other visitors, none of whom I had seen before.

They talked with Iskender, whose Arabic was the best of our party. After they left I always asked Iskender what they had said, and he told me, or at least as much as he thought good for me to know.

All of my fellow-prisoners did their best to keep me from getting alarmed. When there was any extra shouting to be heard in the *bazaar* and I asked what it meant, they were always ready with some good excuse. All the same, I know that they too expected the house to be rushed at any moment, then our fate could be imagined. The cry of 'Shut the door and keep the bar up!' was repeated almost hourly. The sentries were constantly going out and leaving the door ajar, and were most indignant when they came back and found it bolted. That door was the terror of my life. It opened in the centre, and had a wide gap in it, large enough for the barrel of a rifle to be put through. There was just a wooden catch to slip up and down, and a bar of iron, which had to be fixed each time the door was closed. Many times all our hearts, I am sure, stood still for a moment, when a stray shot rang out in the road or someone came and banged on the door, shouting to come in.

Once, I remember, there was a terrific panic in the street. Everyone seemed to be rushing, and yelling as he went. I ran up to the room above, pulled down the shutters, and looked through a chink in the wood. A man came running along and knocked loudly at our door. As he was fully armed, I need not say that I was terrified, or for what I thought he had come. There was much shouting between him and our two sentries inside. I kept crying, 'Don't let him in, don't let him in!' But the iron bar had been taken down, and he was already in the house. I called to the others to come up. They called back, however, that it was all right—only another sentry had come to guard us. I was not at all reassured, especially as shots could be heard in the town, and ran downstairs, feeling that it would be safer to be with the others.

In spite of their calm behaviour I could see that they were secretly uneasy. I asked Baines whether he thought the tribesmen had broken into Shahraban and were coming to kill us. Oh no, he said, it was only a scrap in the town; the Arabs always panicked like this. I accused him of pretending that things were all right, so that I should not be frightened. But he persisted that there was nothing to be alarmed about. To judge by his composure, there could not be much, and I felt that he was the right man to be near if death were at hand. The others were cheerful enough, and their talk was comforting. But Baines's courage was the most infectious.

Nothing further happened beyond the arrival of the third sentry. This, however, seemed to upset the other two. All three began quarrelling, but fortunately they did not come to blows.

In the evening Sheikh Hamid came. He began by asking if I was better, and did I want anything. Only clothes, was my answer, for we had enough food now. Iskender had advised me not to ask for clothes, as it was useless. Anything the Arabs liked they would never give up. (They had evidently taken a great liking to everything of mine!) Still, I asked, and he said he would see if some could be obtained for me.

The *sheikh* told us that he was changing our guards as the three we had now could not agree. The new arrival had been a Kurd, and did not get on with the Arabs. Four new sentries were coming that night. He assured us that we would be safe, and nothing would happen to us. He told Iskender to tell me that it was not for the sake of the British Government (which he did not like) that he was seeing that no harm came to me, but for the sake of Major Barry, who had treated his women with such respect. At that time I had no idea who Major Barry was; but I liked Sheikh Hamid better for his frank statement.

As he left, he assured me again there was nothing to fear, that he was in Shahraban often, and would come to see us whenever he came. He really succeeded in making me feel safer, while he was there; but after he left I very soon began to get 'nervy' again.

Not long after, Abdul Khalis arrived, actually bringing with him a sewing-machine, needles, cotton, a pair of scissors, a toothbrush, and two rolls of bandages, one for Baines and the other for me. Baines certainly needed bandages, for all he had had to dress his wounds all the time were the same old ones, washed out and dried. I had had to do the same. My sores were getting worse and spreading, in spite of the great care I took in bathing them daily and keeping them covered.

Abdul Khalis told me that it was his sister who had lent me the sewing-machine. (It was not mine from the billet, I could see.) I was very pleased with it, and started making my dress at once. I had waited long enough, to be sure. I cannot say that the dress turned out a success, but at any rate it gave me something to do.

My dog Scut had now found me out in my new prison, and was most faithful—at meal-times! He was a dear dog, in spite of being such an utter mongrel, and missed very much the games I used to have with him, asking very plainly for me to get up and chase him about. I was feeling far too ill, however, for that kind of thing now.

CHAPTER 23

A Variety of Visitors

My narrative has become rather scattered, I fear. But the fact is that, though I was now in freedom compared with what I had experienced at Sheikh Majid's, and also knew now the days of the month, I was in no condition of health to keep a proper diary. I was quite alive to all that was going on around me, but could not at the time have brought myself to write down the day's events, even if I had had a pencil. So I must tell the happenings as they occur to me, until I get a definite date again.

One day we had some very strange visitors. First there were two tall eagle-eyed men, fully armed, whom I was sure were tribesmen, though Iskender said they were not. Then an Arab who had been head of the police under Captain Wrigley, a very alert little man, dressed in khaki and a *fez*. He had a wonderfully decorated dagger, terribly sharp and keen. This I noticed when he handed it round for inspection, and I thought that nothing could have resisted that steel. Lastly there was a young Arab, very gaily dressed, with an exceedingly bright *kafiyah* bound like a turban, with fringe and tiny tassels hanging from it. Iskender and the others talked with these visitors. The man with the turban eyed Iskender nearly all the time, only throwing occasional glances at the rest of us. Iskender sat apparently quite calm, but moistening his lips with his tongue from time to time, as was his habit when perturbed.

The visitors did not stop long. The moment the door was closed, Iskender let forth.

'All lies!' he exclaimed. 'Nothing that they have said is true!'

'Tell me, Iskender, what was it all about?' I asked.

'Nothing—all lies!'

'You *must* tell me,' I insisted.

154

'Oh, they have said the British are never coming, and the tribes-men are getting stronger and stronger. You saw that man with the turban? He wants to kill me. My heart was going like this all the time. . . . And the lies that they told, how the British were being defeated everywhere!'

He was very agitated, but only, I think, because he had been obliged to sit and listen to the men's tales. I told him that I had not noticed that he was afraid at the time.

'No, I would not let him see it,' he replied.

Strangely enough, these men's stories only had the effect of making us think that the British *were* coming. We were so convinced that the men had been telling falsehoods that we took it as a good omen. 'But if the British *do* come, we are sure to be killed first,' I put in.

'They would not dare to kill us, for they know what it would mean for them,' said Baines—and this comforting statement they all echoed.

When I think now how lightly the town of Shahraban has been treated, I do not see so much force in that argument as I felt at the time!

We talked like this for hours. There was nothing else to do but talk. The two Indians and Iskender would have heated arguments about their respective countries. I seem to see them now—the pleasant-faced Mr. Thomas in his khaki shirt, breeches, and *putties*; Mr. Dean in white shirt and trousers; Iskender in Arab dress, all with the enthusi-asm of young men (none was over twenty-six, I believe), praising their native lands, their music, art, antiquities, buildings, etc. Their conversa-tion was intensely interesting, and their descriptions most graphic. The Indians could answer any question about India offhand, with dates; and Iskender had wonderful tales to tell of Egypt. I could listen by the hour, and was quite sorry when the run of the conversation changed. Baines and I were not well enough physically to hold forth about our country; and, anyhow, the others seemed to know just as much about it as we did, and their dates were much more precise and certain.

Sometimes the topic would change to the love-affairs of the Arab women, about which Iskender would wax eloquent. It appears that they do have love-affairs, in spite of their secluded lives, and that wives sometimes run away from their husbands even among the Arabs. Iskender always had an excuse for damsels in distress, and would add with a sigh, 'Oh, but she was very beautiful and loved much! 'What happened when they got old and ugly, as Eastern women so soon do,

I could never make out.

Great discussions would take place about the people in Baghdad, and our political administration was freely commented on. How clearly the Oriental seems to see into our natures! These men had taken stock of everything far more quickly and accurately than I should ever have been able to do, though I am of the same race as the people they were criticising.

There was a lot of talk, too, about Baqubah and the refugee camp there for Armenians and Nestorian Christians. It was evident that the camp was heavily besieged, and that there was much fighting going on. At least, news was brought in almost daily that tomorrow it would fall. And then, one day a very depressed-looking figure came in to see us. At first we all thought that he was an Arab, but he told us that he was an Indian, bearer to the D.I.O. of Baqubah. He alleged that his *Sahib* had gone off when the fighting began and, though he promised to return and fetch him, had never come back. The bearer had narrowly escaped with his life, had been taken prisoner, and was brought to Shahraban.

The days were almost always the same in this billet where we now were. The terrors were certainly less severe and varied than at Sheikh Majid's, but the general monotony was similar. We awoke early, about five o'clock. Tea was brought me by Gosdan while I was in bed. The others sat on another part of the roof and had theirs together. Then I went to wash and tidy myself in the room allotted to me as a dressing-room, while the men went downstairs. When I came down I would find my camp-bed brought down and put where the courtyard was shaded by the overhanging roof. Benches were set alongside my bed, with a table in the centre. Here we would sit and talk all the morning. Sometimes an Arab would come in, bringing anything but cheerful news.

Then one of the guards would bring *tiffin*, supplied from a house nearby, where nearly all our doles of one *rupee* four *annas* were spent, with the exception of what we spent on cigarettes. After this, if there had been no big excitement during the morning to talk about, I would go into the cool room and bathe my horrible sores. Then came a rest, or as much as was possible; for very often there were commotions from the sentries outside, and calls from the courtyard of 'Who is it?' and 'Keep the door shut and the bar up!' These always made my heart thump, though the men always shouted to me that all was well, and we were not about to be killed. I knew that they were not too certain themselves how long life would be spared them.

In the evening, when the sun went down, my bed and the benches were carried on to the roof, and we would all sit round and talk. Later another meal was brought, and afterwards the sentries brought their mats on the roof and lay down to rest, their rifles always by their sides. Often we sat and talked very late. All the events of the Qeshlah were gone through many times. The only point on which we could not agree was whether Captain Bradfield had his tunic taken from him or not. They all said that they had seen it dragged off him. But that could not be the case, for when I saw him after he was killed his tunic was still on. I remember that distinctly.

The story of the finding of the chest of *rupees* at the Qeshlah was thrilling. The excitement had been so great when the Arabs broke it open that they fought like demons around it. One man, as he helped himself to a liberal share, had got his head inside, when the lid was shut down suddenly and his head was almost severed. So his chance of enjoying the loot vanished!

Mr. Thomas, Mr. Dean, and Iskender got away from the Qeshlah almost immediately after it had been rushed. Iskender escaped through the door at the back, against which the car had been pushed, but all his clothes were taken from him before he got very far. Now when relating the story he kept saying, 'Oh, I was *so* ashamed when I passed any women!'

This statement of Iskender's verifies the fact that the townspeople were implicated in the rising and joined the tribesmen. Otherwise, had the townspeople and tribesmen been hostile to one another, no women would have been in the streets.

During the whole of the time I was in these men's company all were more than nice in their behaviour to me. There was never any question who should have the best of everything; it was always given to me. When our cigarettes were almost exhausted, they always insisted on my having the last one. Baines was most unselfish. He refused even to have the loan of my bed for a good night's rest, and continued to sleep on the ground or on a coffee-bench.

How I had dreaded the idea of being put alone with these men! And now how grateful I was for the change! Two were Indians and one an Egyptian, but I do not think that any party of Englishmen could have been more chivalrous to me in every way than were these men; and in writing this narrative I must perforce leave to the imagination of the reader a hundred and one little privations which were lightened

157

CAPTAIN J. T. BRADFIELD.

by the delicacy and thought shown me by my fellow-prisoners—of whom only one was a Westerner. My nerves were almost shattered, and dysentery had a firm hold on me, and I really think that it was the combined kindness of these men which brought me through alive from my captivity.

One night a very unwelcome excitement came to disturb us. It must have been late, as we were all asleep. Firing suddenly started very close at hand. Shots whizzed clean over the wall of our roof. I awoke with a start and immediately rolled flat on the floor for safety. The others called to each other, and the guards snatched up their rifles and ran downstairs. Iskender was very frightened—I think he would have admitted this—and so was Mr. Dean; but not so much as I was. Baines merely asked what it was all about and did not get up. He really could not have known what fear was. Mr. Thomas hurried over to me and told me not to be afraid. 'Don't go, don't go,' was all I could exclaim.

'It is all right, lie on the bed,' he said. 'The shots won't come through the wall. I will stay here.' So he stood between me and the shots, calling to the others to keep quiet, as it was nothing. I knew that this was only with a view to comforting me. But the firing was at such close quarters, and now the continual '*ping*' of the bullets overhead was terrifying. I crouched on my bed, pulling the quilt right up to my eyes, which were fixed feverishly on the stairs.

Our guards had opened the door below, and would not shut it, in spite of being told many times to do so. Any minute, I thought, men with bare swords would dash up the stairs; and there was no way of escape. Though I knew that Mr. Thomas would not leave me, I kept on begging him not to go.

At last the guards rebolted the door and came up to the roof. They looked over the wall towards the town, and seemed very agitated. They told us that the tribesmen were in their gardens, stealing their dates. One man had been badly wounded, perhaps killed. Only one! By the firing and noise I had thought that scores were being shot down on either side.

The firing went on for a long time, but not at such close quarters. Gradually it grew fainter in the distance, and then we all began to talk. The first thing that Mr. Dean and Iskender said was, 'I wasn't very frightened. Just at first, perhaps—it was so sudden!' Mr. Thomas, who had not been frightened, or at least had shown no signs of it, said nothing. I always noticed that, after Baines, Mr. Thomas was the least agitated when there was any cause for fear. As for Baines, he was splendid. He never got excited or lost his head. Perhaps it was due to the fact that he had gone through the war and had grown accustomed to the sound of bullets at close quarters.

That reminds me that I have not said much of Baines's wounds. They were getting better, very much better in fact, and were beginning to heal, but without closing. I sometimes caught glimpses of them while they were being dressed. They were terrible gashes, though they were going on well now. He could move his left arm up and down; the right was still in a sling and useless. The Arab doctor was terribly rough, and must have hurt him badly. All that Baines would say, however, was, 'Steady!' Sometimes there was an intake of breath when a wound was being probed before the 'Mobile oil' was applied—that was all.

One night the women from Sheikh Majid's house all came to see me. Our one and only hurricane lamp had no oil in it, so we were compelled to sit in the dark on the floor of my 'dressing-room.' They all kissed me, for the first time, and how I hated all those horrid wet kisses! As they were now my guests, I felt that I had to make conversation, and called to Gosdan to come in after a while and interpret for me.

The women professed great anxiety about my health. This amused me, for I had been just as ill when I was with them, and it had not worried them much then. They told me how sorry they were that I had gone away from Sheikh Majid's house, as they had all liked me so much. What could I reply to this? I thanked them, but told Gosdan to make it clear that I had not left them because I wanted to go, but because I had been sent away against my will.

While the women were with me, I realised how awful was that eternal chatter of theirs, and sincerely hoped that I should never have to go and spend another day of my life in 'women's quarters.' Before I had actually lived among them, and had only paid occasional visits to Arab women, they had interested me. But now that I knew them and their ways, all the glamour which I thought had been there had vanished.

When they had stayed what seemed a very long time (it was perhaps half an hour) I began to think they were never going. I made a pretext to go and fetch more cigarettes, and slipped away to the men to ask how long they were likely to stop, and what was customary in such matters. Could I ask them to go, or must I wait till they went of their own accord? The Indians said it would be best to make some excuse, to say that I was very tired and wanted to go to bed. I went back, and we smoked and talked a short while more, when, fortunately, they thought it time to go. The kissing began all over again. Ummi was particularly enthusiastic, which was most unpleasant.

At last they went. They were escorted back by a son of Sheikh Majid whom I had never seen before. It appears that he had quarrelled with his father and had gone away, I suppose, until the storm blew over. He had now returned. He was very like Jumeila, and one eye was hopelessly crossed. As soon as my visitors were gone, I began washing my face very thoroughly, to take the kisses off! Besides, I did not want any more germs than I could help.

When I was alone, I appreciated how quiet this place was in comparison with Sheikh Majid's.

Another visitor whom we had was Sheikh Feisul, Sheikh Hamid's brother. He seemed very worried, and told us that he had great trouble with his household. He had five wives and seven daughters, but no son until just this day. He had quarrelled with the wife in question and turned her out of the house to go back to her father. Now that he heard that the child was a boy, he wanted the wife back, and to effect this he would have to go and appease her father. He evidently did not relish the idea.[1]

He had already decided the child was to be called *Balujah* (Trouble!).

Iskender explained the situation to me fully after Sheikh Feisul had gone. I could not understand, however, how the *sheikh* had ever turned his wife out at such a time.

Iskender had many tales of the Arab women, not only of their love-affairs. He told us of the wife of one of the tribesmen who had been fighting against the British. He apparently got tired of the dangerous game, and went back home and told his wife he wasn't going to fight any more. 'Give me your *abba* and sword and horse,' she answered, 'I will go and fight in your place!' He was so ashamed at this that he went back to the fray.

So, with all their faults, Arab women are certainly brave!

---

1. An Arab may give sentence of divorce to his wife twice and take her back, but if he does it a third time, he cannot take her back until she has married another man and been divorced by him.

CHAPTER 24

The British Arrive

We were nearing the end of our imprisonment, though we did not know it yet. We could not help noticing, however, that the whole of Shahraban was in a state of great excitement. Then rumours began to come in that the British were advancing. One curious result was that a great deal of hurried building was suddenly commenced in the neighbourhood of our billet. In particular, a new mud wall was being erected quite close to us. What it was for, I could not imagine. Obviously it could not be turned to any account as a defence. I believe that the real explanation was that rifles had been buried beneath it.

One evening, after there had been a lot of riding through the *bazaar* and the town, town-criers were sent out, calling on all the women to make bread for the tribesmen to go out and fight the British next morning. (This is the scanty equipment the Arab requires when setting out to war—arms, ammunition, and a few rounds of bread and some dates tucked somewhere in his clothes!) Clearly the townspeople and tribesmen were at one again. Immediately a hum arose from every house. Millstones were grinding away everywhere. The call was eagerly responded to.

Our plight seemed a very precarious one now. The tribesmen were in the town, and could easily kill us if they wanted. But would they, if the British were advancing?

That night we all heard the sound of big guns in the distance—real guns this time! The noise was indeed welcome, and we all grew very excited. The other prisoners said they would go out and meet the British when they entered the town, as they would not know in which house we were. They were very hopeful and cheery; but for me, I realised sadly that the British had come too late.

Lots of people came to see us that day. Their manner was now very different from what it had been. All professed great anxiety about my health, and asked what they could do for me.

Sheikh Hamid was among the visitors. He was, though I was not aware of it at the time, on his way to fight the advancing British. He asked if I wanted anything. I said yes, clean clothes. He at once gave orders for them to be brought to me. Later a trunk arrived—one of my own—but when I opened it there was nothing of use to me except a pair of stockings and a bottle of liquid boot polish. Nearly all the other things were parts of my husband's clothing, the sight of which upset me very much, and I broke into sobs when I found a snapshot of my baby John at the bottom of the trunk.

I told Sheikh Hamid that the trunk contained so little of use to me. He said he was very sorry, but that was all that had been given up.

Still, the stockings were an acquisition, for what I had at this time were all holes and almost footless. And when Mr. Thomas had blacked my white shoes for me with the liquid polish I looked nearly respectable.

In the afternoon an aeroplane came over Shahraban. We all ran up to the roof to see it better, but very quickly a sentry rushed up after us and hustled us down at the point of his bayonet. We came down rather subdued, but full of hope, nevertheless, and sat in the courtyard talking. In the short time I had been on the roof I had seen a lot of people on the minaret, all looking towards the fighting through field-glasses. Rescue must indeed be close at hand. Perhaps now it would only be an hour more and then the British would be in the town!

We were very pleased with Mr. Thomas, for he always prophesied that the eighth day of September would be our day of release, and now it was the 8th! We credited him with second sight for knowing the day from the beginning. We talked and talked, and our excitement grew. The men were eager to set out to meet the British when they entered. I was not at all so anxious, for I thought it more than likely we should be shot at on the way.

Town-criers could be heard calling out in the *bazaar* that the tribesmen were being defeated, but that all hearts must be brave. Stray riders were galloping out to join the fray. The sound of guns was growing louder, and we knew now it could not be long. We spoke of what we would like to do when the British arrived. We agreed that we would like to go round the houses with a party of Gurkhas, collecting our belongings and administering to the inmates their due reward!

We were very closely guarded that day. But once I managed to slip up the stairs alone and look out of the window to see what was happening in the street below. There was a great deal of noise, and I wanted to know the reason. I got on to the roof and looked over the wall. The built-out circle round the minaret—the *muezzin's* gallery, I suppose I should call it—was crowded with figures, all intensely excited, gesticulating and pointing in one direction, where a great column of smoke could be seen rising. One of the sentries had discovered my whereabouts and came hurrying up to me, telling me to go down. I was very indignant and told him to go away, which to my surprise he did. He waited at the top of the stairs, however, and I went down very soon, not at all liking the look of his bayonet.

The day seemed to drag on endlessly. At sunset the firing had almost ceased, and we thought that it meant the British were soon entering Shahraban. We sat on the roof that night as usual, and about midnight we lay down—but not to sleep, I think, for our excitement was far too great. Soon a loud commotion arose in the courtyard below. We heard struggling and the voice of somebody calling on Allah. Angry shouting followed, and then a door banged. We were all wide awake and wondering what it meant. But the sentries would not tell us that night. Moans and supplications seemed to be proceeding from the 'snake-room.' No one ventured down, however, to find out the cause.

We were awake early, and eagerly discussed the sounds of the night. Nobody knew what had happened. I, at any rate, would not go down first. Then an aeroplane passed overhead. Iskender told me not to signal in any way, so I lay still. But it was a good sight to see that machine! It was the forerunner, I told myself, of the British column coming for certain today.

When we got downstairs a voice arose from the 'snake-room,' begging for water and invoking *Allah*. The door of the room had a padlock on it. One of the sentries came and passed some water through the bars of the window. Curiosity impelled me to go and look. There I saw a dirty-looking tribesman. We asked the sentry many questions, and it appeared that the man had been in the town during the night with evil intent, and had been caught and put in the prison-house. It was indeed a 'prison-house.' What a collection—two British, two Indians, one Egyptian, one Armenian, and now an Arab! It was well I had not known that the last was in the same house as I during the night, otherwise I should not have dared close my eyes! Not that he appeared to have much fight left in him now. He looked, as I had so

164

often felt, just waiting for the end. I tested the padlock. It seemed quite strong, for which I was grateful. Even now, though the British were so close, I had horrid thoughts of the man breaking out and murdering me.

Presently there was a great rush in the street outside, and Sheikh Hamid entered in a violent hurry. He was, as a matter of fact, fleeing before the British, though I did not know it; but I could see that he was terrified. Still, he bade Iskender tell me that all would be well with me, although he could not stay, as our force was overwhelming and the British would be here in an hour.

His actual words, Iskender told me afterwards, were: 'Too many soldiers, great guns, aeroplanes, horses, and an armoured train. No use trying to fight this!'

The *sheikh* asked if I would give him a chit to say that he was not in Shahraban at the time of the rising, but only came back afterwards. So I wrote a chit, saying he was not, to my knowledge, in the town on the 13th of August; but I ended very abruptly and just signed my name, for at that moment a huge shell whizzed right over our roof. Sheikh Hamid took the note quickly and went off.

I was truly frightened now. So, after all, the British did not know we were in Shahraban, and were shelling the town! After the long agony of waiting for our rescue we were to be killed by our own guns! I told Baines not to forget the messages I had given him for my people. I still felt sure that he would be saved; but for myself I only expected death.

We sat together for a few minutes, none of us speaking, only making an exclamation as a shell passed close. How awful those minutes were!

Outside someone began to bang on the door. 'Don't open it,' I cried; but it was open already, and Sheikh Majid entered with some other men. He said that I must come with them at once.

'Oh, Baines,' I appealed, 'what is this for?' Barnes said they were only taking me back to Sheikh Majid's house, and it would be all right. I had no time to ask any more questions.

The Arabs kept saying, 'Quickly, quickly!' and I was dragged by the wrists and hurried out of the door. I remember that Sheikh Majid held me on one side, and on the other a man with a big wart on his face.

Back through the streets we went. Very few people were about, and I observed that all were without arms. They smiled at me and followed us up. It was a very different crowd from that which had surged round me before—just a lot of peaceful-looking townspeople, without a weapon among them. I only noticed one man on horseback, who was undoubtedly a tribesman. He was fully armed and rode close to our party, glaring at me, with his rifle pointing perilously in my direction. I began crying, some words were exchanged among the Arabs, and with a savage pull at his horse's bridle the tribesman galloped off towards the open road leading to the fighting.

I was brought to Sheikh Majid's house, but not taken to the women's quarters. A mattress and pillows were put on a bench, and I sat down. A number of men then came in, all of whom *salaamed* me. Sheikh Majid stepped forward with some others, and asked me to write a note to be sent to the British, which one of the men would take with a white flag. I was to say that I was here, and to beg them not to shell the town. I inquired for Iskender, and when he arrived I told him what the Arabs wanted me to do. 'I would like to see the town shelled,' I said—'but not till I am out of it!'

'Don't put that,' Iskender answered, 'it will be read. Just say that we are in the town, and that the people do not wish to fight, so will they please not shell it.' So I wrote:

Mr. Baines, Iskender, Mr. Thomas, Mr. Dean, and myself (Mrs. Buchanan) are in the town, at the house of Sheikh Majid. The townspeople are now unarmed, so do not shell it.

This note was eagerly taken. When it had gone, I wished heartily that I had added, 'till we are out of it,' in spite of Iskender's advice.

A great number of men now came clamouring round me, all asking for a chit to say that they were good men. My answer to all of them was, 'The British are very just.' If I said this sentence once, I repeated it at least fifty times. Others came saying, 'It was I who found you and brought you here. Give me a chit.' To this my reply was: 'I will tell the British when they come.' By the number of men who came forward claiming to have brought me to this house on the 13th I might have had a small battalion as escort.

I had no doubts now that the British were coming, and as conquerors too. The friendly looks and greetings which every one gave me were sufficient evidence. I ignored them all. I despised the way in which they were trying to curry favour with me. The only man who came and *salaamed* in an ordinary manner was Abdul Khalis. I just said, 'Thank you, Abdul Khalis.'

'Madam, I am repaid,' he answered, *salaamed* again, and went. I know that, if it had been in his power, he would have done more for me than he actually did.

Coffee was next made and brought to me, while everyone exhibited great anxiety to put more pillows for my feet or back. Sheikh Majid inquired if there was anything that I especially wanted. Yes, some clean clothes—I wonder how many times I had asked him for these! He went off with his son Hassan to get some. Could it be that some were actually coming at last? Presently he returned and said that he was very sorry, but all my things had been buried in different gardens, too deep to be got at now.

Iskender came and sat near me. Noticing that none of the rest of my fellow-prisoners was visible, I asked him why. He said that Mr. Baines had suffered too much already in Sheikh Majid's house and would not come back to it. He himself was returning to Hassan Agha's soon.

'Well,' I asked, 'do you think everything is safe now? They won't kill me now the fighting has ceased, will they?'

He assured me that I was perfectly safe now. I had said in my note to the British in whose house I was, and in consequence they would have to produce me. I almost felt at ease at last, and, though at other times I had been full of terror when sitting among the Arab men, I had now no fear at all.

Someone came and asked me what I would like for *tiffin*. Absent-mindedly I said, 'Chicken and vegetables.' My surprise was great when, a little later, a chicken and some fried tomatoes and rice appeared, and with them a tin of cigarettes. 'For me?' I exclaimed. I could not believe my eyes or realise, until I began to eat, that I was actually getting a proper meal at Sheikh Majid's house. While I lunched, the *sheikh* and another notable of the town sat straddle-legged on a bench opposite me, and conversed in low tones. All I could understand was that there had been many deaths, that Sheikh Hamid had departed hurriedly, and that there was a lot said about the two British prisoners.

I suddenly remembered the letter which I had written and hidden in the stables. I went through to the women's quarters to look for it. Immediately all the women rushed at me with open arms and wanted to kiss me; but I made my escape to the stable and looked in the place where I had put the note. It was gone! Then I hunted on the floor and among the straw.

As usual there was a little group of women waiting for me at the door. They were most anxious to know what I had lost. I assured them that it was only a hairpin!—and gave up the search. I had a look, however, under the pile of mattresses in my former room. As I had expected, the rifles that used to be there were gone.

They did not want me to leave their quarters, and made me sit down, while dates were brought me to eat. Hamid was sent for, and began a long tale of how sorry the women were that I was going. Keremah's baby appeared and was put very much to the fore. The women said that they knew that, as I had lived in this house so long, they had nothing to fear. Would I tell the British how they all liked me and how I liked them and their children? It was pretty evident that the shelling had frightened them as much as it had me!

Jumeila told me that I should have some clean clothes; Sheikh Majid knew where they were. 'Yes,' I answered, 'but they are buried in the garden, and he can't get at them.'

'Oh!' was all she said; and changed the subject quickly. Was I very glad now the British had come?

'They come too late for me, Jumeila. My *Sahib* is buried here.'

With this, I began to cry. There was a groan all round, and some of the women started crying too.

A message came that I was to go back to the men's quarters. When I returned, Iskender was back again and told me that there was not long to wait now. Everything was very quiet in the town. Not a shot was to be heard, and no one carried even a dagger. Sheikh Majid, however, still had his apparently harmless-looking stick. The minutes seemed to creep along. I wished I could have gone with the others to Hassan Agha's house. There would have been someone to talk to then. Here Iskender was busy in conversation with an unpleasant-faced Arab.

Strangely enough, I felt very calm. No thrill of excitement went through me at the thought that release was so near. But when at last an answer was brought in to my note, I did feel a thrill. I eagerly opened the message and read:

Mrs. Buchanan, Shahraban.
Your letter received. A letter is being sent by bearer to Sheikh Majid and Hassan Agha Zingana, informing them the town will not be shelled, provided you are sent out to join the troops immediately with Mr. Baines, Iskender, the A.P.O.'s accountant, and the six other Indians with them, and provided no further opposition from the town is met.

168

(Signed)

34th Brigade.[1]

I tucked the message away in my dress and walked up and down a little. I felt now that I could not keep still. Sheikh Majid told me that we should soon be in British hands. We would go out in *arabanas* to meet them as soon as the sun began to set. The time now must have been about three o'clock. I sat down again, and coffee was brought in for me.

Even at this eleventh hour, however, there seemed treachery afoot. They asked me how the letter was signed. Was it from a division or a brigade? For the moment I could not think which was the bigger; and of course I wanted to say the stronger of the two. I nearly said 'Brigade,' thinking it sounded more imposing, but fortunately I managed to get out, 'I cannot remember, I have torn the message up.'

'Where are the pieces?' they asked. But, despite all their efforts to make me understand, I refused to be intelligent, and only indicated that I had torn it up and thrown the pieces away, with which they had to be content. It was no doubt lucky that I was able to evade their curiosity; for who knows what they might have been planning?

After long waiting, I was at last told to come. I put my hat on and said I was ready. Scut was with me again, obviously well aware that something was about to happen and most anxious to be off.

Sheikh Majid took me aside and, with the help of Hamid, assured me that if the British had not come, he himself would have done everything possible for me. He would have taken me to Baghdad— and more, he would have escorted me back to England and handed me over in safety to the British government! I knew what these fine words were worth, and I reflected how all the time in his house the little essentials I had begged for had been denied me. I recalled how, when I asked for a piece of fine string or cotton to wind round my wedding-ring to prevent it slipping off, as my finger had grown so thin, even this was refused!

Iskender and Mr. Thomas arrived and said that they were going with me to join the others at Hassan Agha's house. I went to the door of the women's quarters, and called out, 'Goodbye, Jumeila!' There was another rush of the women in my direction, but I quickly shut the door again and went over to the men. I could not bear the thought of those women's kisses and their insincere anxiety about me now.

---

1 A similar message was sent to the other prisoners, who had also sent out a note.

169

CHAPTER 25

More Delays; but Free at Last

As we went out, townspeople stood by, smiling and silent. Could these actually be the same men who had gone to make up that yelling horde which surged round me and made that journey to my billet, only a short time ago, such a ghastly nightmare to me? In each doorway that we passed nothing but smiles was to be seen on every face. When we came to the house of Hassan Agha, the courtyard was packed with Arabs, and in the midst of them were the rest of our party. We were all here, I noticed, and it was only a question of waiting for the *arabanas*. The sun was still fairly high, and I think it must have been about half-past four.

Hassan Agha came and told me that his Persian wives would like to see me. I had no desire to see them at the moment; but still I went in. They invited me to sit on a big, high double-bed, with little wicker railings all round except for a space at the side left through which to get in and out. I climbed up and sat down on the bed while tea was being prepared in a big brass urn. Hassan Agha came in and talked a lot with us. I could say little, except on the thought that kept running in my mind: 'The English come too late for me; I leave my *Sahib* behind.' He then began to speak about my husband, saying how good he was, how everybody liked him, and how sorry all were at what had happened. I was crying now. So was Hassan Agha; and so were all his womenfolk. If only they had not stood so close to me, I could have borne it better. But they were clean; and their house, like their courtyard, was totally different from Sheikh Majid's.

Then I was told it was time for me to go back to the others. The *arabanas* were waiting, and it was time we started. We all left the house together, the other Christians as usual forming up round me. As we neared the *bazaar*, it seemed as if everyone in Shahraban must have turned out and collected to see us go. The *bazaar* was crowded on either side with Arabs, unarmed and eminently peaceful in appearance. They seemed to be standing on raised tiers to get a better view of us.

There were three *arabanas*, just plain, primitively-made carts, with flat wooden bottoms and slanting sides. The wheels looked very insecure. In the first, which was drawn by three horses and driven by an Arab, were put Mr. Baines and myself, sitting on the bottom, Iskender, Mr. Dean, and Mr. Thomas. The last-named sat at the back. He alone had managed to secure those most essential things, a rifle and ammunition, which he did by borrowing them from one of our sentries!

The second cart took the other Indians (including some who had turned up at Shahraban from various places) and Gosdan. In the third were some of the Shahraban people with rifles and ammunition, to 'protect' us on the way.

After about twenty minutes' waiting we started off through the *bazaar*, our cart swaying from side to side. Crowds swarmed round us all the while. As we reached the gates which had been built up round the town, our driver whipped up the horses till they were almost at a gallop; but in so doing one of the wheels caught in the side of the wall, and we were all thrown sideways. Poor Baines's arms had been hurting him already, and this made him wince with pain. The horses were backed, and the cart disentangled, and we got out through the gates into the open road. In front of us ran men carrying white flags, to show the British that it was a friendly party arriving.

I looked towards the graveyard where Billy was lying, and wanted to get out; but the others would not hear of this. I realised, when I saw the square little low mud wall, and not a single cross inside it, that the graveyard too had been looted. Just simple little wooden crosses had been all that had marked the last resting-place of some of our men who had fallen in the war; but they had all been pulled up and destroyed. With what object? I could see nothing of new mounds, for the wall cut off the view.

On we went, past the Qeshlah. The main walls were still standing, but everything else had been burnt. The roof had fallen in, and every scrap of iron had been removed. I cannot describe my feelings. The memories crowded back on me. Surely, I thought, we would avenge the outrage that had been perpetrated there!

None of us spoke. The others were watching on either side for any sign of attack. But I turned my eyes back to the little graveyard and watched it until the walls were blurred and indistinct in the failing

GATEWAY OF THE QESHLAH AFTER THE SIEGE

RUINS OF THE QESHLAH

light.

The journey made me realise how thin I must have grown. I could not sit in any position long, and my bones seemed to be coming through my skin. Thank goodness, the British were only two miles away. We had come almost a mile, and so were half-way to safety. But, as we neared a clump of trees, the runners came dashing back in a panic, calling to us to turn quickly. This clump of trees was full of tribesmen, who were waiting to shoot us as we passed! We did not need to be told twice. We seemed perilously near those trees already, and our driver turned and slashed his horses into a furious gallop. Our *arabana*, being the first in coming out, was the last going back—and how we rushed! The road was full of holes and deep ruts, and the cart swayed first to one side and then to the other, throwing us about. I could see that poor Baines was in agony. But what was to be done? Any second a volley of shots might ring out around us.

After what seemed an eternity, we at last neared the gates of Shahraban again. They were thrown open. The *arabanas* rumbled through.

So we were back again—for how long? We all alighted, Mr. Thomas helped me along, and we went up the narrow path by the garden where I had hidden, over the canal, past the coffee-shop, and once more to Sheikh Majid's house. I went straight through to the women's quarters and pulled out a mattress and lay down. I don't think I was frightened. Despair was clutching me, and I began to think of all the things that might happen to us before our rescue could be effected. Though the town seemed disarmed, there were still enemies between us and the British column, so there would be more fighting, more delay; and perhaps the town would be shelled again.

The other Christians had gone back to Hassan Agha's again. There was nobody, therefore, to talk to. My bed was put on the roof, and my bath prepared as it used to be. The women showed great eagerness to be nice to me, and kept asking if I was better. Quite late I was told to go to the men's quarters. But I said that I was already in bed and too tired to go; and they did not insist, which surprised me.

Scut slept at the foot of my bed that night, and in spite of many growls he failed to alarm me. I was beyond even that now! I slept through the night without waking once. When I awoke next morning, I pulled my bed into the shade, took off my petticoat and asked Gosdan to get one of the women to wash it. On such occasions I was obliged to stay in bed and under the clothes until the garment was dry. I was consequently still in bed when Sheikh Majid came up to the

173

roof and said I must get up now, as Major Hiles was waiting for me at the gates by the Qeshlah.

Major Hiles! I had heard that he had been killed in Baqubah, but that was evidently false. I called for my petticoat and asked Sheikh Majid to go away, as I wanted to get dressed. I did not wait till the petticoat was dry, but got ready in double quick time. At last really I would be free today!

As soon as I was dressed I went downstairs. The women all wanted to kiss me, but I managed to evade it somehow. Then Sheikh Majid returned and told me to hurry. I asked where Mr. Baines and the others were. All gone, he said; they went at once, directly they heard. So I hastened to follow.

When we were outside the house, someone came up with an umbrella and held it over me all the way. I thought of the many times when I had needed it far more and it had never been brought me. But, of course, they were anxious to impress on the British how well I had always been treated.

We went past our billet, by the coffee-shop, and through the *bazaar*. Sheikh Majid warning me constantly to hurry. But I did not feel that I could do so, even at that moment when freedom was so close at hand. I was too stiff after the ride in the *arabana* the day before. All the time the strangest calmness was on me. . . .

Not a soul came round us that morning. We walked the whole length of the town without meeting more than, perhaps, a dozen people in all, and they were intent on their own business and took little notice of us as we passed them.

At last we were out in the open road again. I saw a car coming towards me. As it neared us it stopped, and Major Hiles and Major Bourdillon got out and saluted me. I suppose that to many this would appear to be the climax. I have been asked, 'What did you do, throw your arms round them, jump for joy, or what?' No, I did not do anything Like that. I only looked at them, and the words, 'Too late, too late,' kept going through my mind.

Then someone said, 'I'll take you back to the train.' We got into the car and passed the gates of Shahraban. I asked to get out as we drew near the graveyard, and went swiftly over to it. I heard steps, as of someone running after me. I hurried on faster. Then a voice said: 'Cheer up, Mrs. Buchanan. It is all over, we're rescued now.' It was Mr. Thomas. We went in together through the little opening into the graveyard.

Five newly erected slabs of mud marked the place where our five British men were sleeping their last sleep. I looked long, and at each I thought, 'This is yours, Billy.' I fell on the place that marked the grave, and kept whispering, 'Billy, Billy, come back, don't leave me, Billy.' Nothing stirred, and only my sobbing broke the stillness.

Mr. Thomas said, in a very choked voice, 'Come away, don't stop any longer.' But I wanted to sleep there too.

The car came over the stubble, and Mr. Thomas helped me in. We went on till we came to the Qeshlah. Here I saw Mr. Baines and got out again. I wanted to speak, but could not. All I could cry was, 'Baines!' Mrs, Buchanan, it's all right, we are safe now,' he said. I could not answer, and he understood and left me. I went through the passage, straight to the room at the back. The floor was in lumps and all uneven where the roof had fallen through. Nothing else was left to show that there had been any trouble there. It looked so different now, with the light streaming through.

The yard was bare. Of the Ford car only the iron framework was there, the rest having been consumed by the flames.

I went back again to the barn, and stood there in the corner, where I had stood with my husband on the 13th of August.

Then I heard my name called, and went out. There I saw General Coningham, who was in command of the relief column. (I afterwards heard him spoken of as the finest man in Mesopotamia.) I was taken back to where the train was standing. What a wonderful thing any part of our army is! Here and there were groups of soldiers on the lookout. Then a line of Sikhs on the march towards Shahraban. And as we neared the train, lines of remounts, guns, all kinds of equipment. It gave me a thrill of pride to see this marvellously organised column of ours. What a contrast to the Arab going out to battle with only his rifle, his ammunition, and his bread and dates stuck in his clothing!

I was put in a carriage in the train, and washing materials and everything I wanted were brought. Magazines were sent in to me, and then came an astonishing breakfast. At least, so it seemed to me then. There were bacon and eggs, bread and butter, and delicious tea. I drank lots of tea, but found it difficult to swallow anything else, nice as it looked, and foodless as I had been so far that day.

Then I lay down to think; but my mind was too distracted by the excitements outside. A plane was flying low above. Men were galloping up and down past the train. Transport was being piled on wagons drawn by mules. Part of the column was making its preparations for entering Shahraban. And all this was going on with the hot sand underfoot and the blazing sun overhead.

I will just break off here to give a short account of how our rescue was carried out. This is based on the official reports issued by the War Office, and I have added nothing to them.

It was on the 6th of September that one column, consisting of the 34th Brigade, under Brigadier-General F. E, Coningham, left Baghdad (or rather Baqubah) in a north-easterly direction; and on the following day they reached Abu Jisra without opposition, repairing the railway and telegraph lines *en route*. On the 8th they encountered opposition four miles north of Abu Jisra, and forced the insurgents back to the line of the Morat Canal. This was turned by our cavalry, and the insurgents, estimated at six hundred, retired some to Shahraban and some to the south-east. The night passed quietly, and the next day, the 9th, our column reached Shahraban.

A second column, under Lieutenant-Colonel Greer, had set out from Quizil Robat on the 5th of September, with the object of operating from the north-east in the direction of the 34th Brigade.

Thus it would appear that Shahraban (little as we prisoners knew it) was the objective of two rescue columns; but it was the 34th Brigade which actually effected our rescue.

THE RELIEF COLUMN ENTERING SHAHRABAN.

SHAHRABAN (FROM THE ROOF OF OUR BILLET)

CHAPTER 26

Farewell to Shahraban

On the day of my rescue several people came to visit me in my railway carriage. A statement was taken from me as to the occurrences at Shahraban. Then I was asked if there was anything that I particularly wanted of my former belongings in the town. I inquired if any of my clothes could be recovered; and later in the day some of my boxes arrived. I opened them anxiously. No doubt the contents had once been my clothes, but everything was in an awful state now, and hardly recognisable. All the trimmings had been ripped off my frocks, etc. Everything was dirty, and what remained was so torn and wantonly damaged that they were useless. To one black frock evidently no one had taken a fancy, and it was undamaged. One of my husband's brushes was all the silver that was returned. Altogether, everything that was of any service to me could have been put in a small suitcase. The rest were oddments, including a number of odd shoes and a quantity of tattered underlinen.

I made the best change of clothes that I could in the circumstances, so as to be as presentable as possible. After nearly a month of living in the same things, day and night, in that great heat, with only the possibility of an occasional washing out and rough-drying of a garment, my entire change of clothing was a great relief to me. Only my women readers will realise what a different being I felt when I had finished.

In the evening I went back to our old billet in Shahraban, with General Coningham, so that I might identify a townsman, one of the many who had been in the Qeshlah on the 13th of August. The billet looked very changed from what it had been when I was last in it. It was now the headquarters of the 45th Sikhs, and the courtyard was full of men, while the officers were using the rooms upstairs.

The prisoner was brought in. He gave me a sickly smile, poor wretch; and I could not help wondering whether he had a wife and children who would miss him. I hardened my heart, and remembered that no one had lavished such thoughts on me when I was robbed of him whom I had loved best. There were many charges against the man, all of which he denied, constantly exclaiming, 'I? I?' as though he were really the most virtuous man on earth. The evidence against him was conclusive, however, and he was condemned to be shot. The official report states that 'on the 11th (September) one of the murderers of Mr. Buchanan was tried and executed.' As a matter of fact, the man who shot my husband, a nephew of Ali Al-Hilal, of the Beni Tamim tribe, was at large when I was in Baghdad, and to my knowledge still remains so, (as at time of first publication).

Before I left the billet I went on the roof and took a last look round the town. I saw it with very different eyes from those with which I used to gaze on it formerly. What before had seemed beautiful and picturesque now appeared a desolate and monotonous stretch of mud roofs without any enchantment about it. All the glamour had departed.

When we passed through the hall of the house on our way out, a line of inoffensive-looking Arabs was waiting, their whole bearing the very reverse of what it had been during my imprisonment. Then we went through the town, and I passed through the gates of Shahraban for the last time, leaving my dead with no cross or mark to show where the finest type of British officer had fallen. . . .

It was growing dark as I got back to the train, and lamps had been put in my carriage. A doctor came to attend to my sores. I made many inquiries of him, and he was so sympathetic and comforting about my husband's end that when he had gone I too thought that those who had died fighting, valiant and fearless until Death stretched out his hand to gather them, had chosen the better part. Yet how full of life and youth those five Englishmen had been, and how much of the type so needed by the Empire! They had been taken, and I was left. . . .

The next morning Mr. Baines came along to see me. His arm had been dressed and was feeling easier already, but he was dreading the thought of being put straight into hospital in Baghdad. He intended to kick against this, he said; he had been shut up too long, and besides had had enough of hospital during the war. While he was with me, who should suddenly spring into the carriage and dash around but Scut! I had not forgotten him, though he had been left behind in

Shahraban. I had asked for him to be found and shot. This may sound cruel of me. But I could not take him back to England with me, and I knew that if he remained in the town he would be abused and ill-treated. I told Baines of my wish now. To my delight he said, 'Give him to me. You know I'll always be kind to him,' and so little Scut changed a mistress for a master, and I was inwardly very relieved. After all, Scut was only five or six months old, and it seemed very hard to cut his life short so suddenly.

We talked for some time. Baines's statement had been taken also. We were still talking when a message arrived, saying that I was to proceed to another part of the train, which was returning to Baghdad. And so, at about ten o'clock on the nth of September, I began my journey back to England—which eventually took me just three months.

The train went very slowly all the way. Block-houses had been built at intervals along the line, in which companies of Indian troops were quartered. At one point the line ran in a semi-circle round the old track, where the remains of a wrecked train could still be seen. It took the best part of a day to get to Baqubah, thirty miles south of Shahraban. Here I was met by Captain Bell, at that time A. P.O. of Baqubah, and taken to a billet in the town. On the way through the bazaar a group of Arab prisoners could be seen squatting, waiting for a lashing. All were talking together, apparently indifferent to the punishment which was coming to them. When we arrived at the billet, I found that it had obviously been looted; everything that was possible had been done for my comfort, and I had the best night's rest that I had had for a long time.

Early the next morning Scut arrived at the billet. How he had found out where I was I do not know, for I had left him with Baines at the station the day before. I was very touched by his faithfulness.

The train left Baqubah at 9 a.m., with a plentiful supply of iced drinks for me on board, and arrived in Baghdad at 4 p.m. I was met by the Military Governor and taken straight to the Serai Nursing Home.

Going in another direction I saw Baines, and at his heels Scut, obviously quite happy with his new master.

At the nursing home I was received at the foot of the steps by a nursing sister. She was the first of my countrywomen I had seen for ages, and I wonder if she realised how good it was to see her after my long captivity among those dirty Arab women, with their repulsive and insanitary ways.

I was put in a delightfully cool bedroom, a perfect paradise after the noise and heat of the women's quarters, got to bed, and began my treatment for dysentery and those horrible sores at once. I was now a mere collection of skin and bones, far thinner than I had ever imagined myself to be—in fact, almost as bad as Barkah. I had a good look at myself in the glass, and was appalled to see how my face had changed. I was only able to take a milk-diet; but oh the pleasure of having things nicely served! The sisters were never tired of doing anything they could for me, in spite of the heat, and always strove their utmost to cheer me up.

Every one, in fact, was exceptionally kind to me. I had numerous visitors, and the women were all charming, bringing me clothes and anything else for which I expressed a wish. I wanted to get up after being shut up for so long; I felt it would distract my mind; but at my first attempt dysentery drove me back to bed again.

Most of my visitors were eager to hear all about Shahraban. But the memory was so dreadfully vivid in my mind that I could not speak much about it. The tales brought in as to what had happened were almost believed in Baghdad, though no one had felt quite sure what the facts were. One tale which I found firmly accepted was that Captain Wrigley and I had escaped from the massacre at the Qeshlah, and had remained in hiding in a garden until I sent him out to get water for me, when he was shot. This story was also reported in England, and made it look as if I had consented to a brave man going out to his death to get water for me. I never saw Captain Wrigley again after he followed Captain Bradfield out of the room in the Qeshlah on the 13th.

Then I had been reported to be imprisoned in the house of one Habil Effendi, Mayor of Shahraban; and at another time to be still in the hands of Rais-al-Baldiya, the chief Arab official of Shahraban.

After some time I began to feel better and to ask questions in my turn. I could get no satisfactory answers. Why, I asked, was no help sent to our little garrison, when there were so many troops in Baghdad and so small a relief force would have saved the situation? The plane that came over the Qeshlah on the 13th could not have failed to see our plight. It went back and must have reported at once. Why was nothing done? From other quarters men had been withdrawn from their posts by aeroplane or armoured car. Then, why were all the other women removed from their districts before the trouble arose and only I left,

THE ONLY MEMORIAL OF AUGUST 13TH: THE GRAVES AT SHAHRABAN.

VIEW FROM OUR ROOF, LOOKING TOWARDS THE GARDENS.

without any attempt whatever being made (to my knowledge) for my safety? Was it for political reasons, or was it an oversight? Nobody could say, and there seemed no one responsible.

Every difficulty was put in the way of my finding things out. Charming as everyone was to me, none was able (or should I say willing?) to answer my questions. It became very plain to me that someone, or more than one, had made a big blunder, in consequence of which a number of valuable lives were sacrificed, and nobody was prepared to take the blame for it.

Mr. Baines came to visit me while I was in hospital. It was very good to see him again. Already he looked a different person, and his wounds were healing wonderfully. We had lots to talk about, as may be imagined. It appeared that Sheikh Majid was now in prison, which I was not at all sorry to hear. A fine of 150 rifles had been levied on the town of Shahraban—where they had boasted of 'over one thousand rifles and plenty of ammunition'—four houses had been burnt, the one man shot, and some others beside Sheikh Majid put in prison. So this was considered an adequate punishment for the town in which five British men had been murdered.

I left Baghdad on the 12th of October 1920, and at Basrah said goodbye to Mesopotamia—with what different feelings from those on the day I arrived! How full of hope and expectation I had come, and now I was going for ever, far from my loved one, leaving him to lie in his unhonoured resting-place within the mud walls of the little graveyard of Shahraban.

All the way to Bombay I again suffered from dysentery, so that when I arrived I went straight to hospital for nearly a month.

Then at last England . . . and little John!

Conclusion

My story is now finished—and these are the true facts of the tragedy of Shahraban.

Yet what had struck me in Baghdad struck me still more forcibly on my arrival in England—the astonishing number of false reports which were circulated concerning what had happened at Shahraban and afterwards. It is admittedly true that the details were said to be extracted from the statements of Arab ranks in the levies, and that their narratives were not as clear or complete as could be wished.

The levies who took these tales to Baghdad were only too probably deserters, who had watched from a place of safety the storming of the Qeshlah. Being still in Government pay, they could hardly be expected to give any but a good account of themselves, with such details as would lend it an air of probability. And that 'the levies were loyal to the end, dying side by side with their British officers,' was totally untrue.

Another report was that, 'How Captain E. L. Buchanan, an Assistant Irrigation officer, and his wife came to join the post (at the Qeshlah) is not known. His duties did not call him there, but it is clear that . . . the Irrigation officer and his wife were in the trenches.'

Shahraban was my husband's post, and the orders from Captain Bradfield and Captain Wrigley were the same to us as to everyone else in the service of the government, to come to the Qeshlah for safety. I think it is pretty clear from my story that we had no choice but to obey. What would have been both our fates otherwise?

Then much was said of my good treatment. I suppose that when I arrived in Baghdad in the condition I was in, and reduced in weight from 9 stones 8 pounds to 6 stones 9 pounds, they must have realised that the treatment could not have been so very good after all. But I do not know that any one has suffered for it—except myself!

It is useless for the authorities to say that they had no fear for my safety and good treatment. Our government was a government that at the time was disliked by the Arabs. Our men had been killed, not for any personal dislike, but because they were servants of the government. Then why should I, who was a government official's wife, be 'well treated'? Naturally I was hated for this reason.

A still more serious oversight was the total failure to send any reinforcements to Shahraban before the Qeshlah fell. The authorities in Baghdad could not have been ignorant of our situation. Shahraban is only sixty miles from Baghdad, and the rising in our area was not so sudden[1] that there was not time to rush a few armoured cars to our assistance or dispatch some aeroplanes. Baghdad was well supplied with both.

Yet in Mesopotamia there were no less than 13,000 white troops, and Indian troops bringing the total up to about 70,000. Mr. Lovat Fraser, writing in the *Daily Mail* of the 30th of August, complained that the strategical conception of the Imperial General Staff in Mesopotamia had been to scatter their powerful force in little batches over an area of nearly 150,000 square miles. But it was not a little batch of troops that was in Baghdad, and when the advance was actually made on Shahraban the work was quickly performed.

In a country where the supposedly hated Turkish rule kept fair order with no more than 20,000 troops, it could not be to our credit in native eyes that with 70,000, equipped as the Turks had never been, with the most modern military resources, we were so slow in punishing an outrage like that at Shahraban.

Was this punishment adequate? I assert that the townspeople of Shahraban, or a section of them, first invited the tribesmen into the town to loot and do their worst. (My story, I think, sufficiently shows that the tribesmen were welcomed as friends when they arrived, in

1. I have since my return been much struck by some remarks, which I had not seen before, by Major-General Sir George MacMunn, former commander-in-chief in Mesopotamia. They occur in a despatch printed in the *London Gazette* of the 8th of March, 1920. He spoke then of 'the volcanic possibilities' of Mesopotamia, 'the large number of well-armed tribes between Baghdad and the sea,' and predicted that 'the lawless condition of the country may still result in outrage by small bodies, and we have no guarantee that trouble may not break out in districts hitherto unaffected.' Those remarks appeared in March. On the 1st of July a party of Arabs broke into the prison at Rumeita, on the Euphrates, and rescued a sheikh lying there on a charge of rebellion, killing the guards incidentally.

The files of *The Times* sufficiently show how the trouble went on spreading after this date.

spite of the alarm shown by the early stampede on the morning of the 13th.) Then, after our men had been killed and the Qeshlah and the billets looted, the townspeople quarrelled with the tribesmen and drove them out of Shahraban. When the tribesmen grew stronger, and it was thought Likely they would break in again, we prisoners were put in an empty billet, under no one's protection, so that if the invasion came and we were murdered no one in Shahraban could be held responsible.

As the British advanced, there was a reconciliation between the two parties, and both were united against us. Only when the defeat of the Bedouin was obvious, and their flight before our column began, did Shahraban close its gates against them and make the majority of them go round the town instead of through it. When the British actually arrived, they found a peaceful unarmed population awaiting them.

When an Englishman kills a native in any remote part of the world, he is generally brought to book. Why, then, when Arabs, who when any looting is to be done are worse than savages, murder the flower of our English manhood, is so little exacted in the way of reparation? The moral effect is ruinous. If a severe punishment had been inflicted on Shahraban at the time—it is useless later, for it is well known that the Arab 'sees only with his eyes'—it would have served as a lesson to the townspeople and an example to others, and the outbreaks would probably not have continued as they did so late as last October, when we read of a cavalry reconnaissance from Shahraban being heavily fired on from Amraniyah, ten miles to the south, and followed up by mounted Arabs.

★★★★★★

On the 13th of August 1920 five Englishmen were brutally murdered in Shahraban. Up to the time of writing no intimation has been received that any headstone or memorial has been erected to mark their graves. Is not this alone a cruel slight, in Arab eyes, to our brave men's memories? Will not the Arab say we do not care? No cross shows the place where they lie. Only the pitiless Eastern sun will blaze down through the long years on some unhonoured mounds within the mud-walled cemetery of Shahraban.

I often wonder why I was spared to come through the horrors I have undergone. Who knows if it was not that I might vindicate the heroic sacrifice of this little band of Englishmen?

186